A Spoke in the Wheel

A Spoke
in the Wheel

Les Woodland

Drawings by Johnny Helms

PELHAM BOOKS

PELHAM BOOKS

Published by the Penguin Group, 27 Wrights Lane, London W8 5TZ, England
Viking Penguin, a division of Penguin Books USA Inc, 375 Hudson Street, New York,
NY 10014, USA
Penguin Books Australia Ltd, Ringwood, Victoria, Australia
Penguin Books Canada Ltd, 2801 John Street, Markham, Ontario, Canada L3R 1B4
Penguin Books (NZ) Ltd, 182–190 Wairau Road, Auckland 10, New Zealand

Penguin Books Ltd, Registered Offices: Harmondsworth, Middlesex, England

First Published 1991
10 9 8 7 6 5 4 3 2 1

Text Copyright © Les Woodland 1991
Illustrations Copyright © John Helms 1991

Typeset in Linotron 11/13pt Korinna by PCS Typesetting, Frome.
Made and printed in Great Britain by Butler & Tanner, Frome and London

A CIP catalogue record for this book is available from the British Library.

ISBN 07207 1972 0

Contents

1.

How to start a fad

I was on a training run once, somewhere around Hatfield, when we were overtaken by a Skoda, three men carrying rucksacks and a lady with a Tesco trolley. It can get like that, cycling.

All that effort to become a Giant of the Road – a *géant de la route* – all that misery, hugely wasted. And when you get home, it's to find your mother's elderly relations being disbelieving and patronising by turn. What they say is 'Eighty miles? Gosh, you must be very fit.' What they *think* is (a) 'Eighty miles, my foot; it'd take us all day to do that in the Cortina,' and (b) ''bout time that boy grew up and started going out with girls, surely'.

It is very hard, being a misunderstood athlete. And it's even harder, of course, when you insist on being taken seriously in shaven legs, waxed, skin-tight, crotch-bulging shorts* and a jersey that looks as though it was designed by a seventies drop-out on

---

* This, of course, refers to the blokes. It's quite possible to spend fifty leg-and-mind-shattering miles with a woman in your group without realising she's there. I once rode all round Bedfordshire in the rain without twigging that the elfin individual giving me a hard time on the climbs wasn't a fella after all. The first clue was an embroidered rose on the bum of her tracksuit; the second, but only when we'd

> *finished, was a long pig-tail that fell out of her rolled-up balaclava. Sadly, there are so few women racing that when most blokes meet one, they attribute the absence of a bulge in the shorts not to any difference in sex but to an unfortunate choice of saddle.*

LSD. *You* appreciate that the unknown words running round your chest represent the finest sponsors known to the sport, but your relations, on the other hand, are reminded of nothing so much as the graffiti they've seen in pictures of the New York subway. They go along with the *Detroit Post*, which got hot under the collar about anyone who looked 'as though he ought to be out chopping wood, straddling a two-wheeled toy in the middle of the day'.

In the old days, the only way you could get those jerseys was to wait in the back seats of the Villa Marina while the prizes were handed out towards the end of Isle of Man Week. Word ran among the harder-up professionals from Ghent to Grenoble that there was a fast buck to be made by selling off suitcase loads of redundant jerseys to third-cats who'd come up for the week from Wigan and Watford. As the men with big paunches droned on about the exploits of the week, any jack-the-lad with an ounce of sense was leaping over the back seats, like a film of the audience at a strip show run backwards.

Now, of course, jerseys are run off by the thousand in printing presses all over Europe. When the only way to get a Great Britain jersey was to be selected for a team, there was so much kudos in having one that you wouldn't dream of wearing it in the street. These days you can get as many as you like by sending a postal order to Kettering, so there's no point in having one at all.

Instead, to be a true poser, you have to be a trend-setter, too. You have to join that long line of pioneers who have set the pace before you. It's inconvenient that they're largely foreigners and by and large quite good at it as well, but you have to take your inspiration where you can.

Take Eddy Merckx, for example. When he was riding the Tour de France and getting more and more muscular every time you saw him, he wrote the letters M-E-R-C-K-X across the knuckles of his track mitts. By the end of the summer, you couldn't stop at traffic lights in Macclesfield, or Taunton or who knows where else, without finding someone spindly alongside you who'd labelled his mitts S-M-I-T-H or P-A-L-M-E-R or whatever. It was a harmless sort of trend, and nowhere near as daft as skin hats or almost anything American, but it didn't half upset people with names like Fothergill or Jenkinson or Ranulph Twisleton-Wykeham-Fiennes.

Jacques Anquetil was another one for setting fashions. Everyone thought it was something new when Merckx began drilling holes in his chainrings and hacking off the surplus supporting bits, but Anquetil was there a decade earlier. Frère Jacques would disappear into the shed of his château near Rouen, shake his spare tubs off the Noir et Decker, and drill quarter-inch holes all down his Mafac (*'un doigt suffit'*) brake levers. I don't suppose it made much difference to the lightness but it made a cracking good moaning noise whenever he hit a headwind. The brake manufacturers were

. . . a cracking good moaning noise . . .

tickled pink, of course, because to do the job properly you needed four really neat holes in each lever. You only had to bodge one slightly, which was more than likely, and you ruined the lot. Or the levers snapped off the first time half a dozen pensioners in screw-on hats tottered out of the community whist drive and under your wheels. Either way, you still had to buy more levers, which the brake factories loved. In fact, I'm researching a theory that Anquetil was in on the plot.

It was something I never saw in Belgium (chrono-spatial simultaneity with old ladies, that is). When I lived there, I rode every day from the Dutch border to the centre of Antwerp. Belgium is the most densely habited country in Europe, so the government encourages a rapid readjustment of the population by taking cycle paths down the middle of shopping-centre pavements. At the greatest speed I could muster, the old ladies were fairly safe. But the same paths were used by steaming, heaving bunches of Belgian racing cyclists, stinking of embrocation and looking glassy-eyed. All that separated them from a considerable drain on the national health service was an inch of yellow line down the middle of the pavement.

I was looking through an old copy of *Cycling* the other day when I found a report by one of the old boys of time trialling, a chap called F.T. Bidlake. It was about an attempt on the fifty-mile record, last century, by Leon Meredith. These days, the most popular course for the straight-out '50' is in Wales, where you can sail off the side of a mountain and plunge and plunge until you're into your *plus grand braquet* (or 'top cog', as they say at Boroughbridge). In those simpler times, though, the record was run through the Home Counties, which even then were crowded.

'His "50",' said Bidlake, 'gave me at least a sensation when I saw him sail through the crowded, narrow street at Maidenhead at shoppers' tea-time. He literally hand-assisted people out of his way, he edged through most marvellously, treating the road like a choked track with an expert's skill in shooting through the tiniest gap, determined not to be bottled or shut in from his final sprint.'

This old boy Bidlake was quite a character. Like all racing cyclists before the car era, Bidlake cycled to races and stayed with one of hundreds of sympathetic landladies known to organisers all over the country. Sometimes blokes would sleep three or more to a bed, several beds to a room. They slept, ate, rode, and then breakfasted

... would sleep three or more to a bed ...

again before cycling home. They'd ride eighty miles to the course
on Saturday, race for a hundred miles and then cycle eighty miles
home again after a second breakfast. It was a cross between
religious fanaticism and self-imposed national service, made all the
odder by being up and about when the rest of the world was still
gearing up for the omnibus edition of *The Archers*.

The best tale of those days in general and Bidlake in particular is
one that Seamus McGonagle tells. A cyclist racing in the Midlands
in 1956 'thought he had struck it lucky when his landlady
mentioned that she was used to "racing cyclists' ways". Sure
enough, at crack of dawn, she produced his breakfast: three raw
eggs in a pint of stout! A startled inquiry elicited the information that
her racing gentlemen always had eggs in stout for breakfast.

'"And who was the last racing gentleman to stay here?" she was
asked.

'"The last," she mused, "I think . . . yes . . . I'm almost sure . . . it
must have been Mr Bidlake."'

But to get back to Belgium for a moment, I lived there slightly too late to see Merckx at his best. But it was impossible even then to be both a Merckx and a Freddy Maertens supporter. Freddy Maertens, the eldest son of a cycle dealer from Lombardsijde, near Ostend, won more races than Merckx ever did and became world champion twice as well. But Maertens never made it in the trend-setting stakes.

To encourage Freddy Maertens was akin to being a flat-earther. Whatever the poor bloke did, everyone was after him. If he turned up they jeered; if he didn't, the papers were full of criticism. If he won, it was only because he was a sprinter; if he didn't, folk said his best days had gone. He could lead the Tour de France for days on end until it got to Belgium, and even then the Belgians would be ungrateful. No wonder the poor chap got confused.

Maertens is actually quite a sociable, intelligent chap who speaks good English. Quite unlike most of his workmates, he stayed on at school until he was eighteen, to study economics. But I think even his friends would say he has what I once heard described as 'a special face'. When he gets excited and talks in that funny piping voice, he looks just like an animated sponge puppet. In the end, frustrated by a hand injury that wouldn't heal, Maertens made so many comebacks that it got so you weren't sure whether he was on a new one or still on the one before. Finally, nobody noticed any more, and now he lives with his wife Carine by the sea near Ostend.

Merckx was just the opposite. I've still got an Eddy Merckx key ring somewhere, but I could also have had Eddy Merckx balls of chewing gum (on which the picture made him look very flushed and fat-faced), Eddy Merckx tea towels and, if I'd moved fast enough, a picture of Eddy Merckx's backside.

There was an entrepreneur, the kind of photographer who makes a fortune by waiting for topless ladies to stride through the surf and kiss Prince Charles, who followed Eddy Merckx into the changing rooms at a race near Brussels. There he waited until Merckx's back was turned and his trousers dropped, and took the picture. Within days it was printed on posters, a kind of hairy-bummed alternative to the tennis girl who discovers she's got no knickers. It was very popular – if short-lived. Monsieur Merckx was hugely upset. In fact, he didn't see the joke at all, and he went to court to get it stopped. The silly thing was that it would have been a much better joke if the photographer had taken the same picture of Patrick Sercu. His name, in coarse French, does actually mean Tight Arse.

. . . his trousers dropped, and took the picture.

It would be a very good idea, as you try to make an impression without actually shedding much sweat, to persuade your clubmates to give you a nickname. The best riders in history have always had one. Laurent Fignon, for example, is 'Le Professeur', Bernard Hinault was The Badger ('Le Blaireau') because of his grey flecks. They called Merckx 'Monsieur Merckx' to his face (ie 'Bonjour, Monsieur Merckx' and not 'Ça va, Ted'); but 'The Cannibal' when they thought he wasn't listening. They called him that because he ate up not only all the prizes but all the opposition as well. Similarly, Anquetil was 'Maître Jacques'. The Cannibal is a name anybody would be proud to have. 'Monsieur Hardcastle' sounds a bit over the top, as would 'Maître Colin', but I'm sure you could come up with something good if you tried hard.

But to get back to that training ride for a moment, the one that started the chapter. We'd gone out through Cambridge and we were back on our way towards Hatfield when we realised that not only did we feel dreadful, but that we were moving only slightly faster than the lamp posts. We hadn't eaten, and when that happens, you just get slower and slower until you're brushed aside by the breeze of overtaking charity bed-pushers and marches by militant members of the Pensioners' Rights Association. Not, actually, that it always pays to ride too fast even when you're up to it. Even the stars come to regret it, and I'll give you an example.

For year after year, the Tour de France always stopped the night at Marseille. In fact, packs of Frenchmen had ridden into town every summer for twenty-seven years. It was a great occasion for the town and, in the nature of these things, for all the big-wigs at the town hall. They would turn up, try to remember the names of the cyclists, and hand out the prizes. Until a fateful afternoon in 1971, that is.

It was then that the race had one of its record stages. It thundered through villages where supporters were still in the bars. It hurtled over hills that were supposed to slow it down, and it careered into town like an ice hockey match on wheels. The race finished an hour and a half early. In fact, it finished so early that not only were half the spectators still not there but nor was Gaston Deferre, the mayor for eighteen years. By the time he and the aldermen turned up to confer their blessing, the riders were all in the shower.

Monsieur Deferre was not at all amused. He was so unamused, in fact, that he never allowed the Tour de France into the city again. It had to go somewhere else until the old boy died in 1986, whereupon the Tour organisers weren't going to put themselves out and waited until July 14, 1989, before they returned.

I've always fancied riding the Tour de France. In the early days, you could, of course. You didn't have to go through all the sticky formalities of being quite good at it and joining a team and hoping for a place. You could just sign up and ride, and even when old Henri Desgrange decided he'd rather have teams, he always left a few places for anybody else who fancied tagging along. He called these fellow travellers *touriste-routiers*, which is full of French understatement. So far as Henri Desgrange, the organiser, was concerned, they could ride his race so long as they weren't a nuisance. All they had to do was put their luggage on the train in the morning, ride the race, collect their suitcase at the other end and amble round the town looking for accommodation.

At first, all the journalists also caught the train, which kept their numbers down. The race vehicles couldn't get through the mountains in those days, anyway, and factories would try to get their cars on the Tour simply to show they'd last longer than their rivals'. When they did, and you could be driven about in some comfort, the journalists turned up in numbers. The worst problem they had when they got to the other end was a budding hangover, and they didn't have to stand around at the railway station waiting for the *Étoile Rouge* parcels service to hand back their luggage. By the time the *touriste-routiers* showed up, with aching heads, aching legs and somebody else's suitcase, the journalists had already taken all the spare beds and were down in the bar knocking back *pastis* and pasties. And so the *touriste-routiers* disappeared, which was a great shame. I have often thought Mrs Thatcher might have insisted the French re-introduce them as a symbol of buccaneering free

. . . sleeping the nights in telephone kiosks.

enterprise, but the French have always gone their own way, haven't they?

The nearest I ever got to a *touriste-routier* was Johnny Hardcastle, who was famous across several counties for riding to time trials in full touring gear and sleeping the night in telephone kiosks. He couldn't get his bike into the kiosk unless he took the wheels out, so he'd pull the thing to bits, settle down on the floor and tug in the bike, bags, wheels and everything else after him. The problem was that this left very little room, so that every time he rolled over, all the stuff came crashing down on him, the door opened an inch, the light switched on and he couldn't get back to sleep for several minutes until the timer turned it off again. He managed to several times, but packed it in after he was disturbed at 2 am by a man who wanted to call an ambulance for his pregnant wife. He said disturbances like that upset his form.

But to get back to that training run, I don't think, in fact, that we ever did go training like that again — not without stopping for a rest, anyway. It's a shame, really. It's odd to think that he had all the right ideas and that only the lack of a crusty old bun to keep our energy up kept us from becoming *géants de la route.*

2.

How to be temperamental

Whenever Johnny Hardcastle did badly in a race (which was most times, whether he slept in a telephone kiosk or not) he took it out on the cat. As soon as he got home, he flung his rolled-up spare tub at it. The cat, even though it was only a simple animal, got to realise that a clump behind the ear with a tyre not only meant a detailed result sheet was unnecessary but that it was pretty much an inevitability associated with Sunday afternoons.

. . . flung his rolled-up spare tub at it.

As a result, it would lie about dreaming of whatever cats dream until it got wind of somebody approaching with a funny walk. This it always associated with Johnny Hardcastle in his cycling shoes. It would then flee in the face of impending pain. The cycling shoes were beyond its intelligence, however, so that all it actually needed was a peculiar walk. Pretty soon, the cat was turning tail and scarpering at the first approach of arthritic old ladies, drunks, roller-skaters, most of Johnny Hardcastle's cycling friends, and the boy from the grocer's, of whom nobody was ever quite sure.

Even though the cat was otherwise quite normal, a vet – after a couple of especially disappointing seasons – diagnosed it as prematurely senile, which was a relief to Johnny Hardcastle's mother, who'd been considering having her son exorcised. The cat was put down and Johnny Hardcastle did as badly as ever.

The one thing you could say for Johnny is that he never gave up. His persecution of the cat aside, you never got the flashes of temperament from Johnny that you get from French chefs, moody strip-tease dancers and untipped taxi drivers. Which was a shame, really, because with a little effort he could have overcome a lifetime of never quite winning £3 vouchers from bike shops at the other end of the country. He could have become *memorable*. You can be remembered always for a good paddy even when you've been forgotten for everything else.

Take Pierre Brambilla, for example. There was a man who took the hump in the grand manner, a man to whom flinging a tyre at a cat was as nothing. Pierre Brambilla was an Italian gent who'd been riding (not very well) a Tour de France which he'd been expecting to win. Getting angrier and angrier with every mile, he finally despaired of the whole business, stormed off home, dug a pit in his garden and buried his bike upright (like Mad Jack Fuller, who is buried somewhere in Sussex, sitting upright in evening clothes, with a roast chicken and a bottle of port on his lap).

Classy eccentricities like this follow in the tradition of men like the Baron Pepin, a playboy who took two valets with him to act as pacemakers in the 1911 Tour, and a bloke called Dozel who stopped at intervals to hand out photographs of himself. By 1919 these little flamboyant excesses were being heavily penalised; in that year's Tour, Henri Desgrange set his men off on what is still a record, a 486 km epic from Les Sables-d'Olonne to Bayonne.

Even winning the Tour de France doesn't guarantee a happy life.

... buried his bike upright ...

Fights between riders and spectators are not unknown in bike racing. The most celebrated modern incident involved a Paris–Nice race of the 1970s, during a time of industrial unrest when aggrieved workers frequently stopped bike races for the benefit of the publicity. Partway through the race strikers brought it and more particularly Bernard Hinault to a standstill. Entertainingly, Hinault drew back a fist and walloped the first available striker. The race then continued.

In another much-loved moment, Hinault toppled spectacularly into a ravine during the Dauphiné Libéré. Television viewers voted it their big moment of the year and for all I know they're still showing the same well-worn film of Hinault's legs following the rest of him down the drop.

René Pottier, for example, did just that in 1906 and two years later killed himself. He'd always been famous for never smiling, anyway. In the way they do abroad, they stuck up a monument to him by the roadside (you can scarcely move on some mountain passes without stumbling across memorials to terminally punctured bikies). Unfortunately, two years later, the Tour passed that very spot and Pottier's brother, who was also a racer, burst into tears at the sight of it and couldn't continue.

In those days people felled trees in their opponents' path, or spread nails. Close on thirty riders had to call it a day thanks to a bed of nails in the 1913 race. In an earlier episode, the organiser had to fire his gun to break up an all-out fight between spectators and riders.

. . . or spread nails.

It all started well enough. 'The men waved their hats, the ladies their umbrellas,' said a reporter of the first Tour de France, as it left Villeneuve-St-Georges on the outskirts of Paris. 'You felt they would have liked to touch the steel muscles of the most courageous champions since Antiquity . . . . Only muscles and energy will win glory and fortune. Who will carry off the first prize, entering the pantheon where only supermen may go?'

But by the next year, the winner, Maurice Garin and one of its biggest stars, Louis Pothier, were being harassed on the road and told what would happen to them if they didn't let a local boy, Faure, win at St Étienne. It was later that day, on the col de la République, that the fighting broke out and officials had to fire shots in the air. Next day there were more fights and this time it was the police who fired their guns.

The riders might have been more subtle in their cheating – or some, anyway, as I'll tell you in a moment – but they were just as effective. In 1910, Gustave Garrigou wrote of a stage that went right through the night: 'We were crossing Nîmes-Perpignan for the eighth stage. I took care the previous night, as always, to take my Alcyon cycle up into my room at Nîmes. It might have seemed a needless precaution because our team had so far dominated the Tour. The only scuffling for places was between ourselves. Anyway, I forgot to lock my door, a mistake which cost me dearly.

'We were going through Lunel at about 3 am when my front wheel gave up, ball bearings spilling everywhere. Someone had done a good job of unfixing the hub, and I hadn't noticed a thing. So I had to find a mechanic – at 3 am – then search for bearings of the right size to replace those I had lost.

'To be blunt, I lost an hour and a half over that. And I had been within seconds of (my big rival) Faber.'

I said *most* riders were subtle cheats, but they weren't all, by any means. Garin won for a second time in the second Tour. It took four months of inquiry to work out how he'd done it. Nobody knows to this day precisely what happened, but there were claims of riders with private gangs of thugs, and of riders covering parts of the course by car. Garin and the next three riders were disqualified and had to hand back their prizes.

This left the French in a quandary. Garin was a 32-year-old chimney sweep and – although not because of that – they were very happy when he'd won. He was a Frenchman, after all. When he was disqualified, of course, they had to change back smartly. Luckily for them, it turned out that Garin had actually been born in Italy and had only later acquired French nationality. Therefore, they could celebrate when he won and shrug and blame his foreignness when he cheated.

Temperament of this and other kinds can get you a long way. To the not inconsiderable surprise of several entire continents, Freddy Maertens won the world road race championship in Prague late in 1981. He did it by a very simple tactic. He just spread word that he was dead, which didn't seem an overambitious claim, and spent several seasons riding accordingly. Therefore, when he turned up in the stubborn greyness of the People's Capital, he was able to catch everyone unawares at the end by sprinting very hard in a kind of nose-thumbing ho-ho-ho fashion.

To everyone else, Maertens was a people's hero. To the Czechs, though, he was just another unknown running dog of capitalist imperialism. In those pre-glasnost days, news in the Czecho-slovakian press was a lot more new houses built or an unusually productive day at the local nail factory. To them, the world championships ended with the amateur road race and the final opportunity to have a good day out booing the Russians. So who on earth was this funny little professional man, covered all over in Flemish words that made even Czech look understandable? They neither knew nor very much cared. They applauded politely and then left him to those who knew him better and to the stewarding policemen, whose instructions were that he should go to the podium, directly to the podium, or go to jail.

It was at this world championship that the president of the British Cycling Federation was observed wearing a watch set grimly to British time, a full hour behind what the locals were using. Quite who on the press bench spotted it first will never be known. Nor will the identity of whoever sold the story to that wonderful and now sadly defunct scandal mag, Pro-News.

Certainly, the lady in question, Eileen Gray, recognised the implication that not only she but the whole BCF were behind the times and she spent several rounds of the amateur sprint championship accusing all the journalists in turn. Her principal suspicion fell on the man from the Daily Express, *but since he said it wasn't he who sold the story, I suppose it couldn't have been.*

As a result, Maertens was trapped on one side of the barrier while his wife was one of several thousand jubilant Belgians on the other. Mr Maertens, not surprisingly, wanted to see his wife, and his wife wanted to see her husband. He couldn't see her, but we could all hear her yelling at him with a voice which several seconds later echoed back off the Austrian mountains.

'Freddy!'

'Hoi!,' said Maertens, romantically.

'*Nein,*' said a policeman detailed to keep them apart, trying German as a lingua franca.

'*Da's mijn man!*' Carine was bellowing, as good as ever.

'*Nein!*'

'*Ik wil mijn man zien,*' yelled Carine again. And before the policeman could refuse again, he was interrupted by the unexpected arrival of a large Swiss man called Bruno Wolfer, who was shouting 'Television, television!' at the top of his voice.

Now, before I get round to Wolfer (and this isn't entirely irrelevant), I should point out that not only is Switzerland not an awfully big country, but it's also an uphill kind of place. Therefore, the few cyclists it turns out tend to be thunder-thighs of acceptable talent who are greeted by Swiss standards extremely enthusiastically (ie moderated applause and polite ruffling of the overnight Swiss franc rates).

There are few recorded anecdotes about the Swiss, since they are, by and large, a nation as dull as the Norwegians but lacking the fresh fish. Of an entire nation, only two worthwhile racing cyclists come to mind. The first is Hugo Koblet, a man with a nose so prominent that it appeared he might have inadvertently turned into a cuckoo clock, his nose protruding as though he was forever recording a newly started hour. Koblet was known, thanks to his commendable grooming and his internationally famous table manners, as 'Le Pedaleur de Charme'. And being Swiss, that's about as interesting as the story gets.

It's certainly a more salubrious tale than the one that surrounds a fellow countryman which is somewhat harder to verify. It was current in the days when I worked for *Cycling* magazine and it concerns Oscar Plattner, at that time the national track coach. Oscar, it was said, was so far beyond Errol Flynn in sexual stature that, in the right circumstances, he could accommodate thirteen budgerigars.

'Can this possibly be true?' an admiring journalist once asked him.

'*Ja*,' said Plattner gravely, 'but the last can stand on only one leg.'

Since I have also heard the same story told of the Dutch sprinter Jan Derksen, I'm not at all sure it isn't apocryphal.

At this world championship I stayed at the flat of a stranger who, by the simple measure of stopping me in the street, offered me his spare room. His other guests, recruited in the same manner, were a girl who worked in Moscow and her boyfriend, who lived in London. They met half-way in Prague. 'Why is it,' I asked my host, 'there are queues to get into so many of your shops?'

'Ah,' said Janek, looking hurt, 'I have been to your country and I have been to a big shop you call Tescoss [Tesco]. And there, people queue to get out. What's the difference?'

Anyway, to get back to the world championships for a moment. There we were by the roadside at the People's Stadium in Prague, with Carine Maertens trying to get to her husband, and Bruno Wolfer booming 'Television! television!' at the policeman.

'*Nein!*' he said again and this time rested his hand on his revolver as a hint. Bruno, being Swiss and therefore accustomed to years of neutrality, took no notice. Instead, he thrust his face close enough for the policeman to get the full blast of whatever he'd been eating for the past 160 miles, and boomed 'Television!' for the final time. His voice reverberated way beyond the city; several skiers enjoying unaccustomed early snow outside Zurich were caught in an avalanche, and had to be rescued by the *skipolizei*.

The policeman reeled back, reached again for his gun, and was followed quickly by not only Bruno but his bike. Its front wheel led the rest of it over the barrier, followed by a vast brown thigh covered in small flies stuck in a gritty film of embrocation. The policeman gave up, Carine went through the same gap, and several hundred Belgians dancing the conga and waving Stella bottles followed on.

There was some speculation afterwards that the policeman had been taken out and shot, but I didn't feel strongly enough about it to file the story. Maertens went on to die a more lingering death. He was never the same man again, and a couple of years later, when the world championship was held at Goodwood, he retired from the race and rode into a garage door by mistake.

I have no idea whether Wolfer got his television interview. The usual form is for the host nation to provide the coverage for Eurovision and for each national channel to conduct its own interviews, usually only in sound. Therefore, while Czech television was interviewing Maertens ('Tell me, who precisely are you?'), the Swiss would have seen Maertens and heard Wolfer.

A further curiosity was that while Radio Moscow carried long reports about how the American, Sue Novara, had won the sprint championship a week later in Brno, there wasn't a word about it on Voice of America.

Belgian television commentaries were for many years done by a chap called Fred De Bruyne, who was one of Belgium's heroes and had been periodically called the Lion of Flanders (the *leeuw* being the Flemish cultural emblem). There are more classics in Belgium than anywhere and, being quite long affairs, they stump the mobile cameraman for new angles. Therefore, for variety, or maybe just for a stretch after several hours with a heavy camera on his shoulder, the cameraman would curve forwards and give you half a minute or so of some star's feet going round. De Bruyne, whether he realised it or not, was famous on these occasions for saying 'Look at his feet, look at his feet!' Perhaps there were hidden messages in the pedalling technique.

Eddy Merckx once gave a pair of his shoes to a fan. He was stopped in 1979 on his way to the changing room in Eeklo and asked for the shoes '*waarmee u hebt net gereden*' by a chap who kept a shrine of famous racers' shoes in his bedroom, each fresh (at the time at least) from the race. Elsewhere, on Majorca, a pair of cycling shoes hangs in a shrine at the back of the Palma Cycling Club, as a perpetual memorial to a member who died on a mountain road during the Tour of Spain. They hang silently, draped with a St Christopher, candles burning continuously beneath them.

The wisdom of putting cycling shoes anywhere near heat is doubtful. In 1949, on his first trip to Paris, the old Tour de France *maillot jaune*, Wim van Est, stayed at a hotel the night before riding the Grand Prix des Nations. The race was rated then as the unofficial world time trial championship. Van Est had raced in the rain that afternoon and the hotel *patron*, reluctant to let him keep a filthy bicycle and clothing in his room, offered the use of his boiler room instead. All went well until the morning of the race, when van Est found the Frenchman had left both his bike and his shoes leaning against the boiler stove. His shoes were small enough to fit a pixie and his saddle had shrivelled and shrunk like a chain-smoker's lung. Only a chance meeting with a carload of Belgian journalists provided him with borrowed shoes and a bike with only one brake. They were a poor substitute, but van Est raced all the same and was in the lead when he was misdirected at the entrance to the Parc des Princes track, and finished second.

Van Est, who lives in southernmost Holland, considers himself Dutch by nationality but Belgian by personality. This puts him and his neighbours in a quandary, because Belgians are a good deal more temperamental than their neighbours, the Dutch, and each national views the other with the suspicion and amusement you reserve for people most like yourself. The Dutch regard the Belgians as dim; the Belgians consider the Dutch stolid and mean. To an extent, both are right. At the Ghent six-day, the place is a riot of shouting, with enthusiastic spectators only too keen to clamber over several rows of seats to offer advice to the riders. In Rotterdam, on the other hand, the Dutch sit there monkishly, worrying about how much it's cost them to get in.

A Dutch joke about Belgians. **Q:** *Why do Belgians have windscreen wipers* inside *their cars?* **A:** *So they can drive along going 'Brrrrrrm!'*

A Belgian joke about the Dutch. **Q:** *How did the sand caves in Limburg come into existence?* **A:** *Two Dutchmen were camping and one of them lost a guilder.*

Both these jokes are rather better in translation. In Norway, they say they're the funniest thing they've heard in years.

The first time Eddy Merckx rode a race, he punctured, changed a tyre, chased back, passed the bunch and won a prize. The Belgians, though, wouldn't believe him and said he'd taken a short cut. That's Belgium. Later, of course, they realised their mistake. Still an amateur, Merckx was picked to ride the Olympic road race in Tokyo.

He couldn't have been terribly well known even then because if you look back through the pages of *Cycling* and its report of how the future world champion was knocked off, you'll find him called *Willi Merckx*.

Eddy was born in June, 1945, and he lived in the Woluwé-St Pierre area of Brussels with his parents, who ran a grocer's shop. He came under the influence of his coach, Félicien Vervaecke, and at the age of eighteen – while he'd still have been a junior under the present Belgian rules – Belgium picked him for the world road race championship. His parents couldn't spare the time to go with him, but they promised to watch on television.

'Eddy,' said Mama Merckx, 'you must give us some sign on the last lap if you're going well.'

Eddy couldn't think of a sign, so his mother suggested he should freewheel and shake his legs twice. Eagerly, the family crowded round the screen. Brimming with excitement, they spotted him in the leading group. For an hour they watched and then, on a gentle descent, he shook both legs. They were delirious. Within half an hour they were ecstatic. Eddy Merckx was champion of the world. On the phone, Mother Merckx thanked her son for giving them that sign. Young Eddy was baffled. He'd forgotten all about it. He had shaken his legs because they felt tired.

In the days before television coverage, the Italian prime minister De Gasperi was following the Tour de France on the radio. At the time, Italy was getting deeper and deeper into a political crisis and De Gasperi heard less and less about the race because reporters were being called back by their offices. Overnight, he realised that one of the country's stars stood a good chance of success and a win would take the heat off him. He rang Gino Bartali's hotel, explained the situation and begged him to win next day. Bartali obliged not only that day but on seven of the twenty-one stages, setting a speed record that stood for six years. Italy was astounded because Bartali hadn't won the Tour for ten years. They forgot their political troubles, peace returned and Bartali was received by the Pope.

Eddy Merckx was an extraordinary bloke. Rik van Looy, a great Belgian before him who now helps run Herentals football club and organises cycle-racing classes on Saturday mornings at the town sports centre, used to pull out a spanner, slacken his handlebars and lower them during the race ready for the sprint. Merckx once went just as far by raising his saddle while plunging down a hill in south-eastern France. I once drove up the hill with Jock Wadley, the doyen of cycling journalists, and he pointed out where it happened. The car was in third gear at the time because it couldn't take the climb in fourth.

. . . raising his saddle while plunging down a hill . . .

Things were pretty dull until Merckx turned up because the leading riders were so similar, and their teams neutralised the racing. So Merckx was a refresher. In the 1968 Giro d'Italia, for example, the race approached the Tre Cime de Laverado in the knowledge that not only was it one of the toughest climbs in Europe but also swept by snow. As riders struggled and shivered and stared through the squalls, and as team car drivers turned their wipers and their heaters full up, Merckx just carried on riding.

The Italians have always been obsessive supporters of Italians and rarely anybody else. To them, the spirit of Fausto Coppi lives

Football has always been van Looy's great love. Generally, cyclists are too much like loners to be good at team sports, and in Britain they've often rejected several other sports before turning to cycling. As a result, says the old Milk Race winner and national champion, Les West, cycling in Britain gets a handful of genuine athletes and an awful lot of physiological oddballs, for whom cycling is the only way to disappear among other oddballs.

West himself could have become a professional footballer. Eddy Merckx's favourite sport was not cycling but basketball. Greg LeMond would rather play golf than race on a bike (he only started cycling because a drought in California interrupted his career as an acrobatic skier); and Joop Zoetemelk rode a bike only to prepare for ice skating.

Johnny Hardcastle, like Barry Hoban, enjoys table tennis and will remain the club table tennis champion until the table is returned from the annual road race, where it was used and subsequently broken by the tea ladies.

forever. But Merckx's domination was so complete that a poll by the newspaper *Stadio* showed that of the twenty-one million Italians who followed bike racing, thirty-one per cent thought Merckx the *campionissimo* and only twenty-five per cent still backed Coppi.

Not that luck was always with him. In the Tour de France of 1975, a 55-year-old Frenchman (the age isn't relevant but it's the kind of detail we authors love to include) ran out from the crowd on the Puy-de-Dôme and punched him hard in the stomach. Merckx carried on to the finish at the top of the hill, freewheeled back down, identified his attacker and later demanded damages in court – just one French franc, nominal compensation. The Frenchman was fined £60.

Fans, in fact, can be a dreadful nuisance. Tradition has it that they walk miles and miles up mountains with buckets of water, with the express intention of throwing it over their favourites, to cool them down. This was fine in the days when the crowds weren't so dense, or water was scarcer, or spectators were less inclined to walk long distances with a bucket. Now, unfortunately, they throw so much water that it makes the riders' jerseys both sopping wet and unbearably heavy. And all that weight has to be lugged up the hill, of course.

And the riders don't always want it. Time after time you see them breaking their concentration to fend off enthusiasts who want to push them (for which there's a fine and, ultimately, disqualification) or throw water over them. A fan did Jacques Anquetil no good turn at all when he emptied a bucket over him in the 1966 Tour. The intention was faultless; the execution, however, was doom-laden. The fan threw the water at the very top of the Grand St Bernard pass and Anquetil grew so bitterly cold on the fast descent that he couldn't get his breath. He left the race next morning.

Old G. P. Mills, one of the first stars we ever had, had the good fortune to win Bordeaux–Paris. And as it happens, the next three – Holbein, Edge and Bates – were also our chaps.

But their feeding habits, as so often with the British, puzzled the French. Cycling's *report ('The Great Road Race: Bordeaux to Paris: G. P. Mills Victorious') back in May, 1891, explained: 'Mills' feeding was a subject that fairly overcame the Frenchmen. They seemed to think that G.P. meant making a week's holding at each town, and to see him jump off, stick his head in a bucket of water, bolt a pile of strawberries with terrific rapidity, was something that fairly got over them.'*

It's a tradition in British time trialling to hand up rather than throw water. Like most clubs, we appoint the least able of our number to stand in lay-bys and surprise innocent motorists by leaping out in front of them, and running up the road with an extended arm, ready with a bottle for a cyclist that the motorist never noticed.

The usual fault is to raise the bottle a couple of inches at the very moment the rider reaches for it. Why this should happen nobody knows, but it does. You can send dozens of dry-mouthed riders to their doom this way, and it's not surprising that the best riders rely on their own helpers.

A long-distance man on a stinking hot day in the New Forest during the 1970s probably wished he'd done just that. He'd got to that stage in a twelve-hour race where he willed every traffic light to turn red in front of him. When it didn't happen, he rode on resentfully, an ear cocked for the hiss of a welcome puncture. After close on 200 miles, and feeling worse than ever on the leg back from Salisbury, he spotted a lay-by team with bottles. Feeling hot and exhausted more than thirsty, he sat up, lifted the bottle and tipped its contents over his head as a shower.

Sadly for him, it contained not water but Ribena.

3.

How to be a chap who can't play football very well

Johnny Hardcastle had a friend called 'Back Wheel' Ambrose, who fell in love with every woman he ever saw. Sadly, this was largely a unilateral experience because, apart from other deficiencies, he had eyes veined in deep red from all the grit that had been sprayed into them over the years. The few girls who would go out with him became convinced he was peering at them through diagrams of the London Underground system, and they found themselves inadvertently making small-talk about the Central line. This, of course, flummoxed Back Wheel because, like most other cyclists, his conversation was limited to embrocation, gear tables and the letters' pages of *Cycling*. To Back Wheel Ambrose, phrases like 'a good ride' had only the one literal meaning and his incessant pursuit of women in the face of such repeated rejection was, we could only assume, the result of some inbred hunting instinct.

It was eventually his great fortune to meet an especially myopic girl from Walsall who fell in love with his voice. They bought a tandem together and joined the Cyclists' Touring Club. It was commonly voted a service to humanity that each had saved someone else the misery of being married to the other.

On a damp day in August, 1983, Johnny Hardcastle was best man at the marriage, having ridden a '25' that morning and gone straight to the church, thereby puzzling the cat. It was only at the wedding that we discovered Back Wheel's real name was Nigel.

Sadly for him, Back Wheel's racing prestige wasn't notice-ably better. It was his misfortune that most of his career, if that is the right word, coincided with the rise of 'Thighs' Sweeting. Thighs' real name was Theobald, which wasn't always wise to mention.

Despite hanging on to anybody who'd let him take his back wheel, Ambrose could rarely get to the finish any-where near Thighs Sweeting, the growth of whose legs compensated for parallel atrophy in his brain. After a while, Back Wheel, to save himself the cost of postage and the trouble of riding, offered to pay his entry fees directly to Thighs, since he was going to win them off him anyway.

The nearest Back Wheel got to being of use was to get as close to the finishing sprint as he could and then shout 'Go Thighs!' as soon as he saw the yellow flag. Back Wheel then frequently fell off, which gave Thighs the kind of diver-sion needed to guarantee him the gallop.

You can see the photographs of them all even now, the photographer's flash reflecting off Sylvie's glasses, so that she looks like she's been locked in by Securicor. Three clubmates (the fourth not having shown up, but later sending his apologies) are standing awkwardly in the church doorway, trying to hold an arch of wheels. Unfortunately, one of them is only the schoolboy champion. Being shorter than the rest, and having cycled over that morning before removing his front wheel, his tyre has left a wet, brown smudge on Sylvie's headdress.

But it was a happy day and not in the least spoiled by several more clubmates who arrived halfway through Sylvie's father's speech, entering noisily and unchanged from a wet '100' on the Bath Road. Their embrocation and still-damp clothing cast a curious miasma which only the cyclists present could identify. ('Rather like linen baskets' was how Sylvie's mother put it, when she and the bride's father discussed it later.) The Bath Roaders were grateful to have arrived in time to laugh rather too loudly as Johnny Hardcastle read their telegram, which said 'Don't forget – no licence, no ride.'

... trying to hold an arch of wheels.

Sylvie's mother later asked to have the joke explained, but she was told it was an old road racing expression that would take far too long to go into. Her husband made a speech about Sylvie now being in the club, which neither she nor her mother quite appreciated, and Sylvie's dad was pleased that the joke went down as well as it did at Rotary the previous week.

Finally, the happy day ended with Nigel driving Sylvie to a honeymoon at Alton Towers, in a car which had pale brown marks from the suckers of the roof-rack, and various accessories tied to the back bumper. Among these was the front wheel belonging to the schoolboy champion, who consequently had to padlock the rest of his bike to the church railings and walk three miles home in the rain.

Back Wheel's attitude to women is not unusual among cyclists, who see them either as mumsy types selling tea and collecting race numbers, or simpering blonde hot-shots who grace the sport for a few years before getting moony-eyed and disappearing with a man in a Porsche. Since they're not interested in the first and haven't got the courage to approach the second, your average racing cyclist's view of a woman is that she's a pretty poor substitute for a bloke.

... and walk three miles home in the rain.

'In young girls,' said the *Northern Wheeler* in 1892, 'the bones of the pelvis are not able to resist the tension required to ride a bicycle, and so may become more or less distorted in shape, with perhaps, in after life, resulting distress.'

That old song about 'why can't a woman be more like a man?' applies with a vengeance in cycling. This was never more obvious than when Marguerite Wilson broke the record from Land's End to John O'Groats in 1939 and was described by *Cycling* as 'five feet five inches of sturdy British womanhood'.

For many years, in fact, *Cycling* had a 'ladies' page ('conducted by Atalanta'). It had useful advice, such as 'to ride fast is an accomplishment that few lady cyclists wish to cultivate, but the ability to ride far with ease is greatly to be desired. Quite long distances can be covered without fatigue, providing the correct methods are followed.' Among them is the encouragement that 'it is wise to carry a little sustenance in a handlebar basket', which Back Wheel Ambrose interpreted on Sylvie's behalf as two jam sandwiches and an apple carried and subsequently squashed in the back pockets of his jersey.

One of the most celebrated columnists was Fitzwater Wray, who wrote in the **Daily News** as 'Kuklos'. In his Kuklos annual, he denounced trivialities of the day, like the inadequate gear case – 'laced-up things of bad leather and celluloid ... worse than useless' – and rackets in which inferior machines were made and then sold as apparently private bargains – 'Officer going to Mesopotamia must sell much-loved mount'.

He had endless hints. 'After a clean and successful excision of the prostate,' the annual once advised, 'cycling may be resumed if a saddle is used with a central slot or opening along its full length.'

He urged cycle-tourists to push a mirror between boarding house sheets; if it re-emerged misted, the bed was damp. Damp or dry, nobody should pay more than six shillings for bed and breakfast. Five was reasonable, but less than that risked finding someone else in the bed with you in the morning. It was a strange concern for a man who argued that 'a shirt is good for a week, even when worn day and night'.

... push a mirror between boarding house sheets ...

The last time we saw him, he was walking sullenly round the York Rally with two small and snivelling children, trying to look enthusiastic about the prospect of a secondhand sidecar for the tandem. He had the kind of stooped demoralisation that racing cyclists acquire soon after marriage and, more importantly, parenthood. Of Sylvie, there was no sign.

Bidlake had a view on women. Basically, I think, he was against them. 'Cycle racing for women,' said the old eggs-and-stout king, 'is generally acknowledged [he doesn't say by whom] to be undesirable. The stylish, clever lady stops short of being a scorcher, but if women's races were to be organised, the participants would have to run to their limit, or else make a mockery of racing. And that limit is not pleasant to contemplate . . . the speed woman, dishevelled, grimy and graceless.

'Imagine women dressed for speed, on cycles built for speed, in attitudes necessary for speed, grabbing speed food, taking acid and finishing dead to the world.' Yes indeed. But I do wonder about their 'taking acid'? What could he have meant?

Biddy would have hated Tessie Reynolds. Tessie was a pioneer, an early feminist, who saw no reason why what was good for men shouldn't be good for women. Women didn't have the vote and they weren't even expected to work, but these were too big an issue for a 16-year-old. What concerned her more was that women had to dress in frills and glow politely rather than work up a muck sweat. Modern women have a lot to thank her for in cycle racing.

To put her and the British in perspective, it's worth noting that in 1895 Hélène Dutrieu was a heroine in France because she rode 31.19 kilometres in an hour. (She eventually won the Légion d'Honneur, although for flying, so she was quite a lady.) But Tessie Reynolds had been mocked and despised in Britain just two years previously. Tessie rode 110 miles from Brighton to London and back in eight and a half hours. *Cycling* said her effort caused 'real pain, not unmixed with disgust', not to her but to society at large. She'd ridden (here, all gasp) in trousers and been paced by men. This, remember, was an era when the Women's Rescue League in America was claiming that cycling fostered immorality because women met men, and when Parisians were warned that 'the bicycle signifies the end of womanhood since its use causes serious damage to the feminine organs of matrimonial necessity.'

One of the Cyclists' Touring Club's cause célèbres *was to prosecute a Mrs Sprague, of the Hautboy Hotel at Ockham in Surrey in 1899. Lady Harberton, a big noise in the Rational Dress Society, was on a day out in exceptionally baggy plus-fours and a dignified jacket, and having biked a few miles wanted a cuppa. Mrs Sprague, who'd been much vexed at the sight of 'ladies in tights' scorching on the Portsmouth road, refused her service dressed as she was, in the posh bar, and sent her round to join the riff-raff in the bar-parlour: a great snub.*

Lady Harberton was horrified at having the company of 'two men, smoking and talking' and was insulted. The hotel was a CTC-listed establishment and she got the CTC to prosecute, probably against its will. The charge was that Mrs Sprague had refused to serve a bona-fide traveller.

At first it looked a straightforward case, but at the second hearing Lady Harberton produced a photograph of herself, middle-aged and dowdy 'in exceedingly baggy knickerbockers', which gave Mrs Sprague a chance to produce a snap of the public bar, by now all smart and quite respectable.

The CTC lost the case; Mrs Sprague and Lady Harberton secured a small role in history; and women persisted in wearing trousers.

In those days, Rational Dress was a big issue. In these days, of course, you wouldn't want to be seen dead in it. But at a time when it represented liberation and scandal, and the police were raiding bloomer parties in Chicago, it was gripping stuff. These were the days when the CTC looked like Debrett's and magazines had columnists recording what Lady So-and-so wore on her latest bicycle outing.

The Lady's Realm, for example, took the more traditional, perfumed view. For the *Realm*, women's cycling was much more the way Bidlake would have preferred:

'The extensive gardens have been threaded with a wooden cycle track, conveniently shaded by ancestral trees and commanding a charming vista of flower beds; and the fair cyclists have a continuous concert of nature's songsters during the morning hours . . .

'The great feature of the club is its summer social gatherings, when the grounds, tastefully illuminated, and thronged with beauty . . . are a gay scene.

'At the musical rides, the ladies are trained by an army man to ride to military music.'

A spendid amount of tosh was written around these times, some for, some against. Dr Paraclèse Bellencontre of Rouen, for example, considered cycling much less a danger for women than that dreadful pursuit, ballroom dancing.

Dancers, he said, have 'habitually naked shoulders [which] become covered in sweat, affording open and undefended passage to all pulmonary and catarrhal infections. The waist is locked into its tight prison of gauze, satin and flowers, and the respiratory system fails to furnish the body with blood, being troubled by the air fouled by the flames of the chandeliers and by personal emanations.'

On the other hand, 'a velocipede, be it ever so flighty, would never encourage our mothers, sisters and daughters to wear those scanty dresses of flimsy transparent material . . . designed to entice the male dancing partner looking down'.

Women, of course, have also played a great role in the part of the male and mighty. Lucien van Impe, the little Belgian climber, would much have preferred to stop at home and look after his canaries, his great passion. But it was Mrs van Impe who, tiring of Trill on the carpet, insisted that the little man with the choirboy expression ride a couple more Tours de France instead.

And then there's Mrs Terront, of whom history records just one indelicate fact. Mrs Terront was married to Charles Terront, who was big news in France once upon a time. Terront was one of the first real professional racing cyclists; so professional, in fact, that at one time the British, clinging to notions of amateurism, refused to compete against him. He was also an innovative sort of chap. When, in 1893, for example, he was competing in a 1,500 km endurance race, he ran up against the problem that would confront us all in those circumstances: a matter, as the French newspapers put it, of his physiological needs.

Even at quite a fast pace for the day, a 1,500 km epic would take three solid days to complete. And quite a lot of liquid. Terront's solution was to fit his bike with a large bottle and a length of inner tube, which he used on the move to great effect. Mrs Terront's job was not so much demanding as draining. She had to be on hand at the vital moments to grab the full bottle as he rode by, dash off and empty it, and be back in time for when he wanted it next.

All this delighted the French, who have a curious affection for this sort of thing. But it so dispirited his big rival, a chap called Corré, that he was forced to abandon rushing out of the track to the lavatory every couple of hours and had to stuff a sponge down his shorts instead. Terront, so far as I know, won the race thanks to Mrs Terront, and became so famous that he was awarded a reserved seat at the Paris opera.

. . . be back in time for when he wanted it next.

Thighs Sweeting once became terribly enamoured of a sweet young thing called Amanda Lightbody, who spent a couple of seasons racing with us before failing to join the staff of *People's Friend* and going off to become a missionary instead.

It was a pitiful sight because Thighs would follow her everywhere she went, desperately trying to think of something to say, and occasionally offering her advice at the start of evening '10's. This

Terront wasn't always so clever. In 1878 he turned up at a six-day so late that the others had already ridden fifty miles. What's more, his British rivals were eating on the move, whereas he'd reckoned on hopping off his bike and popping out to a café every so often. The track wasn't banked. That, and the indigestion he caught from running to and from the café, meant he kept throwing up. This amused the crowds rather less.

On the other hand, he could spot a good idea. In 1879 the head of the Rudge bike factory sold him one of the first sets of hubs with ball bearings. The French pooh-poohed the idea when he got back and told him all those revolving bits would slow him down.

They didn't.

was usually limited to 'Just go as fast as you can, Mandy,' but it was well intentioned and Mandy seemed to appreciate it. Over the weeks, her times came down quite respectably and her father, who'd worried about her preferring such odd company, became interested in cycling as well. We didn't see a lot of him because he was big in the fried cod business and had to travel to Grimsby a lot, but he was a generous man and sponsored the evening '10's, which we then called the Golden Crispycod 10-mile Challenge. Thighs usually won every round, being fastest at almost everything he did, and he had to ride home each night with four packets of fish fingers which Mandy had brought out in an insulated bag but which melted into an icy slush in his jersey pockets on the way back.

He and Mandy started getting on very well and when he finally plucked up courage to ask her out, he took her to a bike shop in Leicester, two evening meetings at Coventry track, and the national junior '25' championship on the outskirts of Derby (which they never saw because Thighs mis-read the venue in the Road Time Trials Council (RTTC) handbook). He was just thinking of taking her somewhere really nice for her seventeenth birthday when he was struck down by all the frozen fish he'd been carrying home. By the time his cold had recovered, Mandy had left the club and was going out with a chap in the Fenland Clarion CC. Thighs was never the same again.

Mandy, of course, wore the very tights of which Mrs Sprague would have disapproved back at the Hautboy Hotel. Her mother wasn't sure about them either and preferred what Mandy had worn to ballet classes, and Mandy's dad said it made her look like a theatrical hangman, but they came to terms with them.

When tights finally became acceptable, they were patronised by an all-female club in Newcastle-upon-Tyne called the Elite Ladies CC, which began in 1934. There were only five members to start with, all riding in all-black and skin-tight outfits. Whenever they stopped for tea, they pulled open their saddlebags and sat there knitting for an hour or two. As a result, they became known as the Guillotine Ladies.

It's a shame that there aren't many women in cycling, and that Thighs Sweeting and Back Wheel Ambrose accounted for a few of those there were. Given that there are so few racing, it's astonishing how well they do. It isn't that Bernadette Swinnerton could come

. . . sat there knitting for an hour or two.

second (to an American, to the world's astonishment and subsequent aggravation, since they didn't know when to stop winning) in the world road race in Czechoslovakia; it isn't just that Mandy Jones could become world champion in the road race at Leicester – it's that nearly all the records that British women have scored have been scored by just *one* woman.

At first sight, Beryl Burton does not look like an athlete. She's never had the slim athleticism of runners and jumpers. She's never had elfin looks. She's not even big and butch. The one thing you notice about Beryl Burton is that she looks so very unremarkable. She has short, curly hair and, if there's a typical Yorkshire mum, then she's it. I know (in these equality-conscious days) that this is the kind of description you'd never use for a man, but it's just perfectly true. And yet as soon as she gets on a bike, she is transformed; she locks herself in place, her saddle a little low, and one hand gripping the handlebars higher than the other.

When Beryl Burton took up cycling with the Morley CC, the woman of the day was Eileen Sheridan. Where Burton is down-to-earth, Sheridan looked too dainty to ride a bike. And yet she rode 237 miles in a '12' in 1949, won the women's BBAR (British Best All-Rounder) in 1949 and 1950 and then turned professional for Hercules Cycles. Among her records were 446 miles in twenty-four hours (straight out, not out-and-home) and, in 1954, the End-to-End in two days, eleven hours and seven minutes. Beryl Burton had a lot to follow.

Now, it must be said here that Beryl Burton does not willingly give up. The sermon she preaches is that quitting a race is a soul-softening experience. She's addicted to fresh air – the Burton house is identified by its open windows. She's quiet and confident but she's not big-headed. And she does nothing by halves. She won three national championships in 1958 and never stopped. In the next thirty years, she amassed seven world championship gold medals (five pursuits and two road races), three silver and four bronze; twelve golds and two silvers for the national road race; twenty-five consecutive BBAR titles at time trialling; seventy-two national championships and fifty competition records from ten miles to twelve hours; thirteen gold national pursuit championship medals, one silver and one bronze; and two pursuit records.

There is less competition among women than between the more numerous men, but even so, Burton's hundred-plus championships compare to the men's record of twenty-five by Ian Hallam, between 1969 and 1982. If all her best rides had been in 1974, she would have won the *men's* BBAR. Indeed, something of the sort seemed on the cards in 1967. In those days, men and women weren't allowed to ride against each other. The men would have their race, there would then be a two-minute rather than a one-minute gap, and then the first of the women would start. The last of ninety-nine starters in the Otley twelve-hour at Boroughbridge that year was, as tradition demanded, the favourite, a chap called Mike McNamara. Burton – who'd won the world road race championship only a few weeks previously – was first off among the women.

At other times, time trialling big-wigs had intervened to demand that at least ten minutes separate the 'seeded' riders. But here, although they were only 120 seconds apart, the two big stars weren't in the same race – so far as the rule book was concerned. To everyone else, poor McNamara was on a loser. If he beat Burton, he gained no kudos; it was a man against a woman. On the other hand, he couldn't afford Burton to *catch* him for two minutes let alone *beat* him. Both, given Burton's form and her ambitions, were quite possible. When Burton said she was 'just out for a day's ride to enjoy myself', it was very understated shorthand for what followed.

After 156 miles there were still precisely two minutes between them on the road. At 180 miles, there were no more than nine seconds to McNamara's advantage. At 235 miles, they were lapping the sixteen-mile finishing circuit on which twelve- and twenty-four-hour races finish. And there, finally, Burton passed McNamara.

'Would you like a liquorice allsort?' she asked him.

'Ta, love,' said McNamara, and Burton cruised on by.

He had been pushed to 276.52 miles, nearly five miles better than Owen Blower's national record, good enough to secure him the BBAR; *she*, unbelievably, had been driven to 277.25 miles, twenty-seven better than ever before, and at 7:11 pm that evening, two minutes after McNamara had finished, Burton had pushed the women's record beyond the men's for the first and only time in history. Early next morning she set off to watch another bike race – the London six-day – and in the autumn she went on a cycling holiday in Portugal.

Not at all the kind of woman Bidlake would have liked.

'Would you like a liquorice allsort?'

McNamara ate the allsort, which was his privilege but nevertheless seems a shame. Johnny Helms, who drew the illustrations on these pages, has the feeling that it should have been preserved under glass in a Cycling Hall of Fame. People could then have paid good money to stand in a specially darkened room to see it, and pictures could be taken against the day when only a few sugary crumbs would remain. Even the National Trust might have been interested.

But, alas, it is no more.

4.

How to be a poser

It takes inner strength to be a poser. It's a little bit like being one of those Hare Krishna people you used to see wandering about Oxford Street with shaven heads and shoulder drums; you don't *mind* everybody else thinking you're a pillock if you've got the deep belief that you're not. In fact, it's one of the few absolute certainties in life that posers are always other people.

A lot of people had serious doubts about Graeme Obree when he turned up at the 1989 track championships with his legs unshaven, his bars upside down and his wheels, by his own admission, possibly not following each other. I used to ride around like that when I was ten, but it takes guts to do it when people have paid to come and see you. The fact that he then gave the eventual champion a hard time in the heats made him still possibly a nutcase, but he was a *special* nutcase. He made significant progress in the amiable dottiness stakes by telling *Winning* magazine that, while he didn't shave his legs, he did shave the hair in his nostrils to let the air in better. If he progresses steadily he will, in years to come, adopt that patina of public affection which will allow him to be forgiven for anything. A classic example of this was Michel Rousseau, an enormously fat French sprinter who became so utterly gross, even during his racing career, that he eventually had a go at all-in wrestling.

Word had it that it was to a wrestling bout at the De Montfort Hall, Leicester, that Thighs Sweeting had been planning to take Amanda

. . . shave the hair in his nostrils . . .

It's surprising how many cyclists have tried wrestling, at some time or another. Jimmy Savile spent several years as a racing cyclist and rode in the forerunner of the Milk Race – with dark hair, as Oscar Savile, and with less than conspicuous success. For several years afterwards he regularly wore the kind of tracksuit top supplied to the Viking independent (semi-professional) team. He was pictured in it a lot when he broadcast on Radio Luxembourg and eventually, I suppose, it just wore out. He never made a great all-in wrestler, but at least he tried.

And on the subject of enterprising if shady occupations, it's educational to notice just how many of the Great Train Robbers had close or casual connections with bike racing. That old saying about run-down racing cyclists either making a fortune or going to jail proved true in their case.

Lightbody for her birthday, before he was so cruelly supplanted in her heart by the chap in the Fenland Clarion CC. When Thighs wasn't about, Johnny Hardcastle spread word that Thighs thought it was going to be mud wrestling, which he'd heard about from a friend who'd been on a Club 18–30 holiday. The friend had assured him that mud wrestlers invariably ended up topless which, since he'd never persuaded Amanda to dispense with even so much as her anorak, Thighs thought might have dropped her a hint.

But it wasn't to be. Back Wheel Ambrose rather cruelly said he'd seen Amanda queueing outside the Peterborough Odeon, sucking an ice lolly which, so far as circumstantial evidence could tell, had been paid for by a large lad with a crew cut. The two were linked by their lolly-free hands. Thighs was so angry that his '10' time improved by nearly a minute, but he vowed never again to eat Golden Crispycod fish fingers for fear they would remind him of Amanda.

When I later met her father casting a professional eye over some supermarket freezers, he said she was in some newly emergent African nation, trading old RTTC handbooks and spreading The Good Word.

But sorry, I'm digressing.

There comes a time when you realise that you're never going to be a Big Star, a *géant de la route*. It's best that if this is going to happen at all, it should happen early rather than later, otherwise you waste a good deal of effort. Worse than that, you might well end up persuading people that you are in fact a tuggo and complete no-hoper. If this happens, it's a hopeless case. People have long memories and the only thing you can do is move several counties away and start all over again.

It's all very well being an utter dunderhead if you're like Pedro Delgado, who had such dark sunglasses on at the beginning of the 1989 Tour de France that he dozed off, missed the start by several minutes, and finished the day in last place. Delgado, therefore, was on the verge of becoming a dunderhead. What put him in that baffling middle ground between being a Silly Spaniard and a Poser is that he then rode so fast for the next three weeks that he came third overall. To the Spaniards, that made him a hero if not a winner, and they all jumped up and down until they spilled their sangria. Delgado probably became more famous for *not* winning the Tour de France than ever he did by winning it. Turning up late at the village hall and missing a thirds and juniors road race, on the other hand, just marks you down as a twit. The world isn't at all fair in this respect.

There have been few really great Spanish racing cyclists. Apart from Delgado, in 1988, only two Spaniards have ever won the Tour: Federico Bahamontes in 1959 and Luis Ocana in 1973. This, believe it or not, is a worse record than Luxembourg, which has had four victories (François Faber in 1909, Nicolas Frantz in 1927 and 1928, and Charly Gaul in 1958). Britain, of course, hasn't won it at all.

Even Ireland, still further from the Continent than Britain, and with only a twentieth of the British population, had won once by 1989. Thus we've become reduced to enthusing about anybody who *speaks* English rather than actually is English, or British should I say. Thus it becomes better, in these poverty-stricken times,

---

Cycling's heart is forever in the right place but its blindspot for misguided enthusiasm seems to be BBAR winners. Alan Gayfer, the editor who brought the magazine out of its 1950s gloom, in which period it had shamefully become Cycling and Mopeds, *tried as hard as he knew to tag the nickname 'Cat' to Keith Stacey, the 1965 winner, because he came from Cheshire.*

His successor, Ken Evans, was dedicated to time trialling and should be remembered above all for introducing the Campagnolo '25' championship, a hugely popular series of races which lasted several years until the sponsor withdrew. He did, though, grow vastly over-enthusiastic about a crew-cut and straight-faced lad from Solihull called Anthony Taylor. So far as we knew, Taylor's mother called him Tony, but Cycling *at Gayfer's insistence and Evans' collusion succeeded in changing it to Ant.*

Taylor won the BBAR just once, in 1969, followed by a headline on the lines of TAYLOR FOR WORLD CHAMPION? He was a great time trialist, Taylor, but even the most optimistic shrunk back in the face of such confidence. The only things about the headline that turned out to be accurate were the bloke's name and the question mark.

to have an American win than a Spaniard, an Irishman or several Dutchmen on Raleigh bikes than a Frenchman, and Phil Anderson rather than any other Australian because at least he was born in London. We even got mildly excited when an Australian, Bill Lawrie, beat a perfectly good Briton, Dave Nie, in the national professional road race in 1969. Unfortunately it was only when the race was over that anybody asked what an Australian was doing in our national championship anyway.

I've never known the Americans to show the same enthusiasm for the British, or the French to order a fresh round of Pernods because some French-speaking Belgian (whom the French call '*les frites*') has pulled a trick or two on them. No, this desperation for success by association seems to be largely British and, so far as I can tell, unique to cycling.

Of the two Spaniards who've won the Tour, the most colourful was Bahamontes and the most miserable, Ocana.

Bahamontes was an early talent and would hide away through the flat stages and then emerge in the mountains, sitting bolt upright, pedalling a tiny gear, shuffling, twitching and repeatedly moving his hands on the handlebars. Once he started twiddling for the summit, he was unstoppable. He became known, although not to his mother, as the Eagle of Toledo. Or, simply, Baha. In the early days, though, when there was little chance of winning, he used to hate the dangers of the descent and would concentrate on the climbers' award instead. He won it six times (1954, 1958, 1959, 1962, 1963 and 1964), a record equalled only by the canary-loving Lucien van Impe (1971, 1972, 1975, 1977, 1981 and 1983). On one

The reward for being best climber is a white jersey with a bold red polka-dot pattern. Unfortunately, riders found it so embarrassing to wear, right from the day it was introduced in 1975, that there was immediate speculation that it would be replaced.

The French call it the 'maillot à pois', as though there were such things as red peas. The Flemish, on the other hand, call it the 'bolletjes' jersey or, spoken out loud, the 'bollekes' jersey. If the money wasn't a consolation, that would exactly describe how most riders feel about it.

classic occasion, Bahamontes rode alone to a mountain top and rather than descend by himself and fall off unseen, sat at the top eating an ice cream, waiting for the others to catch up. That's talent and posing mixed up in one.

Ocana, on the other hand, got the order the wrong way round. Once, on one of the Belgian's rare off-days, Ocana belittled Merckx on the road from Grenoble to Orcières Merlette in the Alps. He dropped the Belgian in the 1971 Tour de France by a mind-boggling five minutes. Merckx crept over the line, his face etched with pain and suffering. Ocana crowed that he was the new superstar; that it was he, Ocana, who had belittled the mighty Merckx. Big Ted was not amused.

Next day came the awful reckoning. Merckx had been down to the hotel garage that evening to give special instructions to the mechanics working on his bikes. Journalists got wind of a big story breaking and the placed buzzed with speculation. The day dawned black against a sky as grey as the set of a Wagnerian opera. It was weather for low rolling drums and the distant, eery harmonies of demented sopranos. Big Ted was to take his revenge. And the world knew. Merckx led Ocana on a terrible devil's ride that day, through

... eating an ice cream, waiting for the others to catch up.

cloud and wind and rain-lashed roads. His legs turned unstoppably against the pedals. His back, his arms, his face were fixed in a single moment of concentration. And remorselessly, he ground the little Spaniard off his wheel, exhausted him, humiliated him and then left him. That was Merckx.

Three days later, still exhausted, Ocana went spinning off the road in more rain, falling down the Col de Mente in the Pyrénées. Merckx took the lead back that night and Ocana ended the day in hospital. Within eighteen months Ocana had quit the sport and Merckx went on to greater glories.

(Well, that was quite some story, wasn't it? I should take a breather now, if I were you, before you go any further.)

If you really *can't* do it à la Merckx, you must make every effort to persuade everyone that you already have. You have to become A Legend. Alf Engers was a legend even when he didn't turn up. When Engers was the Eddy Merckx of his day, in time trialling in the seventies, word shot round the start area of a time trial near Catterick that he'd phoned from home to ask which way the wind was blowing. If it was blowing the right way, he'd start the race. If it wasn't, he'd stay in bed. Nobody stopped to think that Engers lived in north London, close on 200 miles away, and was due to have started within the hour. That's the kind of aura you have to try to develop.

But how to do it if, by some oversight, you're actually a no-hoper? Easy. You just have to *act* the star. People these days are so dominated by television and the easy packaging of stars into the little plastic frame of the television screen that they yearn to be in the presence of someone special. If people didn't absolutely ache for a little excitement in their dull lives, why would they ever think of the unlikeliest people as television stars, or go out and buy records by the cast of *Neighbours*? Posing, therefore, is a public service.

The first rule about being a star is to dress entirely inappropriately to the circumstances. On the day you ride out to see an inter-club '25', be sure to ride a bike so brightly polished that it justifies the impenetrably dark sunglasses that you're wearing. The glasses, which should be wrap-around, have two purposes. The first is to make it slightly unclear who you are, just in case somebody recalls the day you brought down the whole bunch in your first road race. The second is so that you can seem to be staring ahead in a silky trance of concentration while at the same time looking all around to make sure you're being noticed.

Never ride fast. Apart from the strong possibility that you can't anyway, it'll break the aura of quiet confidence and poise that has to surround you at all times. You have to steer a line between going over the top and looking like Anybody Else.

Going over the top is to ride a bike that looks like what the motor industry calls a Concept Model. You should divide what you spend equally on equipment and chrome polish. Never buy the very lightest, sleekest, super-fandango widgets from Italy, because you have to give the impression that somebody unspecified is paying you to ride whatever you're riding. Since you're an amateur and things like this aren't supposed to happen, you should always look conspiratorially mysterious if anybody ever brings the subject up.

As a matter of interest, you'll be astonished just how much people get paid for using things they might otherwise not have bothered with. In a conversation once with Frank Quinn, Sean Kelly's manager, I asked how much 'a good rider' might collect for wearing a particular brand of shoes. There is no word in Irish for 'yes' or for 'no', believe it or not, and it influences the Irish even when they're speaking English. So when I asked Quinn if he'd tell me, he said: 'I don't think that I could.'

'But you must have an idea, Frank?'

'I have that, but it's not easy to say.'

I picked the highest figure I could dream of for wearing a pair of shoes. He'd scoff and then I'd get the answer.

'Well, would it be, say, £10,000?'

There was a brief pause before the voice came back from Dublin. 'And the rest.'

Ten thousand pounds and more for a pair of shoes! It is, as Quinn himself pointed out, 'a year's wages for fellas in some parts'. By the time you tot up a bloke like Greg LeMond and figure that he's been paid for the sunglasses, the funny pink hat he wears at the finish, his shoes, the triathlon bars which upset everybody (including Bernard Hinault, who wasn't unknown for a few gimmicks in his own time) and almost everything else that's visible, you realise he's making rather more out of the sport than Thighs Sweeting ever picked up.

Bear in mind two things, though, if you want to be a poser. You have to pick a manufacturer and use one factory's equipment all over the bike. It doesn't matter which, provided you're consistent. Give out signals that you're riding what you're paid to ride, and these guys just made you the best offer. It's not what you'd have chosen yourself, you understand, but . . .

This question of sponsorship can cause problems. Roy Thame, when he was manager of the Holdsworth team, one of Britain's best during the seventies, contrived to secure odd bits of support from all sorts of outside factories. One of Roy's hopes was to kit his riders out in an off-the-bike uniform of blazer, shirt and slacks. How much he managed to get at other people's expense, I don't know, but I do recall he managed to get donations of official team underwear.

Hence the problem. How to provide publicity in return? Various suggestions, such as writing 'This team car is being driven by a man in Y-fronts', failed to attract and they settled in the end for a brief mention (literally) on the bottom of each press release.

. . . driven by a man in Y-fronts . . .

Since you're paying for it, go for one of the cheaper makes that polishes up well, rather than Campagnolo, which works wonderfully but is difficult to get to a good gleam. Then utterly abuse just one item to show your contempt for what comes free, just like tennis players break their racquets over their knees at Wimbledon.

The other thing to remember is never to have more than one gimmick at a time and never have one that has caught on generally. Never pioneer. That rider who turned up in the Tour de France with a kind of vortex cone behind his saddle got his picture in the papers and upset the international big-wigs, but who remembers his name? However, when Greg LeMond took to riding time trials with those bolt-on, lie-down, U-shaped handlebars that the more lunatic triathlon riders use, it was immediately considered Definitely A Thing of the Future, just as lock-on pedals and wrap-around sunglasses had been a season or two previously.

There are borderline cases which are hard to judge. When the American pursuit team arrived at the 1988 world championships with small radios in their helmets so that they could listen to their coach in the grandstand, the officials knew they were unhappy about it but couldn't quite put their finger on why. It might have been the prospect of the Japanese showing up decked out in whip aerials, or the British team careering out of control due to the unexpected breakthrough of several lost mini-cabs and the closing minutes of Dave Lee Travis.

Aubrey Fothergill, our club president, was invited on the local radio station a month or two back, and we all crowded round Johnny Hardcastle's radio at the Bessums 'Best for Radiators' End-of-Season Grand Prix to hear him. The race was still going on, but we'd all packed it in early so it didn't matter. They were playing Abba when we got the right station, and then there were several advertisements for garden centres, exhaust companies and a man who appeared to be selling greenhouses, but whose tape stopped suddenly halfway through. There was a millisecond's pause, and then a very hot young man said 'Hi, it'stwelvetwennytwo, thebigFM, Aubrey'snextbutfirstQueen.' Queen then sang *Bicycle* before the hot young man played two more commercials and then said 'Well hi, Aubrey, I guess it's hard work riding a bicycle, huh?'

Aubrey, of course, was flummoxed. Aubrey, in fact, hadn't ridden a bicycle for as long as anyone could remember (which is how he qualified as club president). But he still had a lapel full of small enamelled badges to prove some connection with the sport. Most of them, if you peered closely enough, had engravings of bicycle wheels, with little wings sprouting from the hubs, and underneath or around the edges tiny legends reading Bexhill Autumn Tints Cycling Club or Desert Rats Wheelers (with the motto 'Wheelfolk Against Rommel'). One even said 'Champion blood donor', which surprised us because as far as we could see most of Aubrey's blood had long since settled in his nose, hastened there by several decades of Guinness with whisky chasers.

'Well, I wouldn't say . . .' Aubrey spluttered after a few plopping sounds of indignation.

''course not, Aubs,' the DJ jumped in quickly. 'But some sexy girls in those little shorts, I guess, huh? Seen this album cover?'

Aubrey, who'd thought he was going to talk about the impact of the council's new roundabout scheme on local cyclists, was clearly being shown an LP cover of hundreds of bare-breasted women astride rented bicycles. (It was the Queen album cover that's on every unmarried cyclist's wall, along with torn-out pictures of Maria Blower and the route of last year's Tour de France. Back Wheel Ambrose had to take his down at Sylvie's insistence.)

'I thought we were going to talk about road safety,' Aubrey fought back, now sounding distinctly uncomfortable.

'Guess we are, Aubrey,' we heard the DJ saying, his next record already running, 'that's in a sec. But first, here's Tina Turner.'

She was halfway through a live performance of *Addicted to Love* when two things happened. First, Thighs Sweeting entered the changing room prematurely, his face angry and mud-covered, his left hand holding a punctured tyre. And second, the thrown punctured tyre caught the radio's aerial neatly in the middle and broke it.

We didn't see Aubrey for several weeks after that and none of us felt like asking how the rest of the interview had gone.

. . . the thrown punctured tyre caught the radio's aerial . . .

5.

How to be an official

Looking back, I can only assume that Aubrey Fothergill was *born* old. Like so many cycling officials, he's become rather like St Pancras station – highly functional, unpleasant to look at, apparently continuously busy and too much of an institution to demolish. No one can say for sure just how old Aubrey is except that, considerable though his age must be, he isn't yet old enough to be a national official of the RTTC.

For many years we assumed that his leather-patched elbows and his little round glasses were the signs of an accountant. Further evidence was the way he wore a thin cardigan with drooping pockets under his suit jacket (which had rows of ball-point pens in

> *To Aubrey's enormous discomfort, little round glasses became highly fashionable in the seventies, thanks to John Lennon. Any decent trendy hurried to copy them, but once the quickest had raided jumble sales and begged spare pairs from their grandmothers, there weren't enough to go round. Aubrey, who still played old seventy-eights of Leslie Saronie and Lenny Henry (the original 1920s Lenny Henry, that is, not the one married to Dawn French), used to call him John Lemming. Poor Aubrey, who never understood why, used to be pestered by hippies waiting for him outside Bank station, saying 'Hey man, how's about parting with the cool shades?'*

the breast pocket) and always thought in numbers (rule number this, course number that) rather than emotions. Ask Aubrey how he is and he'll tell you he's 'a little under par, I'm afraid'.

It turned out, though – and only because Thighs saw Aubrey's name in the local paper in connection with a man sleeping under the canal bridge – that he's a solicitor. What he really wanted to be, but couldn't because of the way the legal system works, was a judge. Unfortunately, it's getting a bit late in life to start all over again and, anyway, they make judges retire at sixty-five when they start getting bad-tempered and batty. With RTTC officials, of course, it's quite the other way round, so Aubrey's hanging on for that instead.

He is also possibly the meanest man we've ever known. His one luxury is an annual seaside holiday on the Essex coast, when he stays in a caravan that he inherited from his mother. He never leaves his 1930s house, in a part of town populated by bank managers, probation officers and struck-off insurance brokers, without first removing the battery from his kitchen wall-clock. Back Wheel, having been arm-twisted into driving him to the coach station one morning, caught him red-handed with the Ever Ready still in his palm. All Aubrey could do was look sage, if mean, and mumble something about 'Many a mickle ...'

This stinginess, though, does have its benefits and each year saves the club a worthwhile sum in postage.

Aubrey's greatest love was what he always referred to as the Open '100'. He organises it with the typical flair and imagination of an accountant. His one innovation is never having to buy stamps. The Aubrey Fothergill scheme of race organisation is to save not only the entries when they arrive in the post, but also the envelopes. These he carefully steams rather than rips open. The envelopes are then attached to the entry forms to wait for classification. When the start sheets are printed, Aubrey puts one in each of the envelopes he's been sent. He re-seals the flap with glue and crosses out his name on the front and adds the words 'Not Known; Return to Sender'. On the back of the envelope he then writes 'From' followed by the rider's name and address.

It's a long job but a satisfying one, he says. When it's finished, he drives round the county dropping a couple in one box, a couple in another, and so on until he's got rid of the lot. The post office doesn't remark on a few mis-delivered letters every so often and merely returns them to whence they apparently came. The riders are a bit puzzled, of course, but since they recognise their own writing and are expecting the worst, they're quite delighted to find a start sheet inside and think no more about it. Aubrey, though, has saved the club 120 first-class stamps. He still has to stamp the result sheets (since he never has 120 ordinary letters of his own which he can falsify), but they all go second class anyway.

In this job of organiser, he insists on referring to himself as the Hon. Sec. In distant days, presumably, officials wanted to make it clear that they weren't being paid for their troubles, which would have contravened the rules on professionalism. Therefore, the word 'honorary' was stuck in front to make it clear they were upright chaps who weren't doing it for the money.

In America, where the idea of doing *anything* without money is apparently astounding, *Velo-news* viewed Hon. Sec. as quaintly British and redolent of portly old buffers in striped blazers and caps at the start of the Boat Race. It therefore rendered Hon. Sec. as Honorable Secretary, which sounds like a cross between Lord's Cricket Ground and the Earl of Lichfield.

Whether organisers are honourable or not, the first racers were certainly gentlemen, chaps who worked (or were more likely supported) during the week and raced at weekends. Because they had nothing to go on, and because the first races were on grass or cinders, they borrowed the rules of athletics. In fact, the Amateur Athletics Association used to run cycling for a while.

In America they held bike races at horse meetings, dangerous bumpy affairs on trotting tracks. Entrepreneurs saw their chance. A board track was built at Boston in 1882 and the great American cycling showman, H.E. Ducker, built a scientifically designed track inside the trotting circuit at Springfield, Massachusetts. The effect was formidable. The mile record fell from 3:20 to less than 2:30. The times were so remarkable that the English press refused to print them. Nine thousand people attended on the first day. After the record was broken, 18,000 pitched up. Towns like Hartford and Springfield closed from noon until sunset on racing days.

In America, particularly, there were good prizes to be won. Riders began relying on helpers and *soigneurs* (although the word wasn't known then), big strapping chaps in vests and wide belts. They were not at all like modern soigneurs, who wear short-sleeved white nylon jackets like hard-up dentists. They were pretty strong on tosh and they would dose their riders with purgatives to rid them of 'noxious crudities'. Their riders mightn't have been very fast, but by golly they were never constipated.

It was only twenty-five years ago that even a mundane Good Friday meeting at Herne Hill drew a big crowd. The appearance of Tom Simpson, Fausto Coppi or Jacques Anquetil drew so many, that papers like the News Chronicle *ran pictures of the bike parking area with the caption 'How do you tell your bike from the thousands of others?'*

The ride home across the Thames was harder than anything that happened on the track. It was essential to ride back through Brixton at something in excess of 30 mph, hoping everyone thought you always rode like that. By Vauxhall Bridge there were just you and your clubmates left and you could collapse in Victoria station for a drink.

Nowadays, far from being beaten up by football-style supporters, spectators at Herne Hill are more likely to die of exposure or even loneliness.

'How do you tell your bike from the thousands . . .'

They were also quite hot on secure clothing. It wasn't at all the done thing to breathe your own sweat, it seems.

'The body gives off certain exhalations,' wrote the authors of *The Art and Pastime of Cycling*, 'and these, being warmer than the atmosphere, must of necessity ascend, and the danger is incurred of reinhaling them. To guard against this, the clothing should fit closely, so that a channel may not be left between the body and the clothing which the air of the clothes can ascend.'

The difference between cycling and athletics is that cycling has always been run as a commercial venture first and a sport second. It's still that way today.

Although sometimes it's done pretty dimly. It costs about a million pounds these days to run a top-class professional team; and very often they fall down on the details. In 1989, Sean Kelly's PDM team contrived to have some of the adverts on their jerseys printed upside down.

Better still is the example in the 1970s of a team in Belgium sponsored by a chewing gum company called Brooklyn. At no little expense, it hired the big man of the day, Roger De Vlaeminck, and let him pick most of his own team. Whatever happens, they told him, remember we want good results and good publicity for Brooklyn. At the first race of the year the team turned up with the name mis-spelled BROOKLIN on their shorts, and it stayed that way until mid-season before someone turned up with replacements.

Even more bizarre was the kidnap of Brooklyn's boss in 1975. By the time the firm had paid the ransom, it didn't have enough money left to ride the Tour de France.

It's not surprising, then, that the money-men were up front when racing moved to the roads. The Paris–Rouen race on November 7, 1869, was run not for the riders but the newspaper *Le Vélocipède Illustré*.

In these days, when the Milk Marketing Board backs the amateur tour of Britain, and Coca-Cola sponsors the Tour de France, there's no beating about the bush. They want you to buy something; the

sport sold its soul to commerce decades ago. But then there had
to be a good motive.

'In order to further the good cause of the bicycle,' said *Le
Vélocipède Illustré*, 'it must be demonstrated that the bicycle can
be raced over considerable distances with incomparably less
fatigue than running. By seeing for itself, the public will be able to
appreciate the real merit of the bicycle which makes a maximum
economy of time and energy.

'Therefore we announce a place-to-place race from Paris to
Rouen, a distance of about 130 kilometres.'

The paper then invited 'all the racers of France and foreign
countries to take part'. They did – 203 of them – and it was won by
James Moore, a vet and a Briton. His bicycle had ball bearings
made by the prisoners of Paris.

The same Moore had won, on May 31, 1868, a 1.2 km velocipede
event in the Parc de Saint Cloud on the edge of Paris, now thought
of as the world's first organised bike race. It was the last time we
British showed consistent superiority in cycling. Moore, a
Welshman, no more than five feet tall and in time the best-paid
professional of his era, wasn't the only Briton in the race. He had the
company of an 'exceptionally strong and well built' lady calling
herself, despite her parentage, Miss America. It was quite common
then to race under an assumed name, a privilege I have many times
longed for.

Efficient though Aubrey's Open '100' is, Thighs Sweeting and I
have promoted some road races over the years which have verged
on the shambolic,* so the circumstances of Paris–Rouen, although
very much more forgivable, give us heart.

The idea was that the *coureurs* would go to the Place de l'Étoile
at 7 am to sign on. They were then to go to the Arc de Triomphe for
the start. By 7.15, therefore, much of the field of 325 had completed
the documentation and were riding round to the Arc de Triomphe
for the start. This confused the crowd which had already started
gathering and they cheered, thinking the race had already begun.
This in turn confused the riders, who'd already been split into two
groups, and the pace picked up. No one was going to stop, just on the
off-chance that he'd misunderstood the rules, and they went faster
and faster until they went rocketing past the Arc de Triomphe. This
was of great concern not only to the officials waiting there but also to
the other competitors, who were either hanging about for the start or

* *The local paper, rather unkindly I thought, described one of them thus: 'The result of the "Best for Radiators" Cycle Race, sponsored by a local radiator company, remains a mystery as we go to press.*

'Thirty-six of the original fifty cyclists made it to the finish, after eighty-two miles, but an inquiry is to be held into why the leading party of riders and those pursuing them approached the finishing line from opposite directions.

'A St John Ambulance spokesman said the injuries were numerous rather than severe.

'The race organisers were not available for comment. The president of the organising club, Mr Aubrey Fothergill, said he could not explain what had happened. He had gone fishing.

' "But I understand that sort of thing can tend to occur in massed-start racing," he said.'

. . . approached the finishing line from opposite directions.

getting changed back at the Place de l'Étoile. Somehow the officials organised a second start for some and a first start for the rest, and promised to readjust the times at the finish.

Nobody had raced over such a distance (130 km) and few had ever ridden so far at all. Jimmy Moore was among many who collapsed at intervals, after riding on stunned by fatigue.* He'd eaten only two sandwiches all day. He fell against a fence, was revived with food and wine, and pedalled like a zombie back through the field to regain his lead. Only thirty-three of more than 200 finished, Moore getting there in ten and three-quarter hours, an average of just more than 7 mph. His prize: a medal, and 1,000 francs (a vast sum in those days). It was mild consolation for the fact that someone later pinched his bike. Equally consoling was that, even twenty-five years later, a motor race over the same course could average only 4½ mph faster.

Miss America was twenty-second, six hours later, winning the prize for first woman.

Moore, who lived from 1847 to 1935, later became world champion and a *Chevalier de la Lègion d'Honneur*. We British

---

* *Another participant was a Londoner called J.T. Johnson. He was doing really well. In fact, he'd been leading nearly all the way, dressed in a jockey's silk shirt, a coloured cap and jacket, kid breeches and gaiters. He had a whip fixed to his bike 'to keep off the dogs'. But when he got to Vaudreuil after sixty miles, he started feeling pretty much like we'd all felt on that non-stop training ride round Hatfield. He flopped against a level crossing gate, unable to talk.*

Whereas Johnny Hardcastle couldn't produce as much as an old bun for us, Johnson had the exceptional luck to be taken first to the stationmaster's house for a meal and a snooze, and then to be picked up by the owner of Vélocipède Illustré, given a swig of brandy and taken back to the good man's mansion. There he was given dinner and allowed to rest his legs before being dispatched back into the race an hour later.

Feeling by now rather better than he had, he hurried up the road and came seventh.

then promptly shot ourselves in the foot. We clung to the idea of sport being an amateur business for men aspiring to be gentlemen, competing for canteens of cutlery and 'prizes of an engravable nature'. By contrast, the French allowed their amateurs to win up to 2,000 francs, a professional sum by anybody's reckoning since it was as much as a French labourer would earn in nearly a year and a half. (When some years later George Mills won Paris–Bordeaux – the French having graded it as amateur at British insistence – the National Cyclists' Union, far from celebrating, grumpily recalled that he was works manager at a bike factory and demanded to know whether he'd paid his expenses himself.)

> *Only inflation during the Edward Heath era ended the British time-trialling custom of winning what the programme described as a '£3 voucher' for first prize. What you got, in fact, was a note from the organiser inviting you to send a receipt for something you'd bought yourself as a prize, whereupon he'd post you enough postal orders to make up the £3.*
>
> *Inflation meant it was no longer possible to buy anything for £3. It didn't mean, though, that prizes were increased until some years later, when the only benefit was that you now got your £3 in cash, with all the attendant risks of being declared professional.*

British riders were invited to the new, monster race from Bordeaux to Paris and they objected to many of the best French riders, including the favourite, Charles Terront (he of the inner tube down his trousers), because they were professionals.

Seven thousand people gathered at the finish of Bordeaux–Paris and convinced the organiser, Pierre Giffard of *Le Petit Journal* that he ought to run a still longer race – 800 miles from Paris to Brest and back. Despite forecasts that no one would ride, he had 600 entries and 206 actually on the line on the morning of Sunday, September 6, 1891. This time Terront was there, unrestricted by British moral superiority. He won by seven and three-quarter hours. He broke his chain, he five times punctured the tyres that his sponsor, Edouard Michelin, had fitted to his Humber. The punctures were usually caused by nails that had fallen out of his countrymen's hob-nailed boots, and it took a Michelin mechanic forty minutes to make one of the repairs, to Terront's anger. He even had to go off in search of a marshal who'd wandered away for a doze. He was in second place at Brest and stopped for just six minutes before heading off again, after thirty-five continuous hours in the saddle.

This time there were 10,000 people in the Porte Maillot to greet the winner. Since then, the professionals have stayed but the British have not. The sport became ever more commercial, not least because neither Michelin nor Dunlop would concede that the other made the better tyre. The following year, Michelin promoted a race from Paris to Clermont-Ferrand. His tyres beat Dunlop's and he pronounced them, not entirely truthfully, to be unbeatable. Many years later, Dunlop stopped making first racing tyres and then cycle tyres altogether. Michelin are still going strong.

By the way, next time you're placed seventeenth in the Bessums 'Best for Radiators' End-of-Season Grand Prix, and you grieve because it should have been sixteenth, spare a thought for the officials. Take the case of the sprinters Michard and Protin, for example.

Robert Protin was Belgium's first world champion. On the track in Cologne in 1895, he was up against George Banker, the 25-year-old son of an American industrial tycoon, and another Belgian, Huet. Banker was far and away the favourite and Protin a first-year professional from Liège. The three of them were lined across the track in the final, with Protin and his neat little moustache closest to the railings. When the judges were ready, they gave the order to the starter, who was so overcome with stage fright that he brought down the flag and poked its stick into Protin's eye.

Banker, of course, whistled round the track and won. Protin, equally, didn't. While Banker was waving his arms about in transatlantic mega-glee, Protin was rubbing his eye, blowing his nose repeatedly and complaining to the judges. For several minutes they gathered earnestly to measure the gravity of the situation. Finally they ordered a re-run. Banker was as miserable as previously he had been joyful.

'I won't ride,' he protested.

'You will,' said the judges.

'I won't,' said Banker.

'So you won't be world champion,' countered the judges. And reluctantly Banker got back in the saddle.

This time Protin won, his eye still bloodshot from its encounter with the stick, Banker demoralised and demotivated. Again the American protested, and this time he started getting a little support.

For months the International Cycling Association, the forerunner of the modern international body, the UCI, fretted over what to do.

'All right,' they said finally, 'we'll do it all over again in Paris.' But only Banker turned up. Getting slightly cross, the ICA huffed and puffed and stamped its foot and said it was getting sick of the whole business, but that it'd run the world sprint championship back where it had started, in Cologne.

Now the Belgian federation joined in, miffed that a whole nation's glory was about to be denied.

'You do that,' they said, 'and we'll leave the ICA.' The ICA wasn't as yet sure enough of its position.

'Ah,' said the judges thoughtfully. 'In that case we'll say your man is world champion.' And so he was.

In all, this friendly but moody man had more than 400 sprint wins. From the time he started at sixteen, to the time he stopped thirteen years later, he became national champion in 1891 (at eighteen), 1892, 1893 and 1894; he won the national 100 km title in 1893, the European sprint championship in 1892 and 1893, and in 1893 became the French open 5 km champion. And in 1895, he broke the world 500 m record in Paris. He died in Liège in November 1953, eighty-two years old.

The unfortunate Michard wasn't so fortunate. He was pitched against an aristocratic sort of Dane called Willie Falk Hansen in the world championship sprint of 1931. After two matches they were evenly matched, so everything depended on the third ride. As usual, they foxed and foiled their way round the track. But when they got to the 200-metre point, Hansen was ahead, with Michard on the outside. At this point the judge, Albon Colignon of Belgium, looked up the track, noted who was where, and switched his stare to the finish line. There was no photo-finish, of course, so the championship of the world, which could be decided in just a tyre's width, depended on his judgement.

What he saw, as he stared at the line with solemn concentration, was the inside rider's wheel flash by with half a length's lead. Grateful for an easy decision in so important a matter, he marked

Hansen down as the winner of two matches in three. What he hadn't seen, but everyone else there that day in the stadium had, was that Michard had switched down the track with a hundred yards to go and had sprinted past Hansen on the inside. It was indeed the inside rider's wheels that had crossed the line first, but they were Michard's and not Hansen's.

In a moment Colignon realised he'd made the wrong decision and sought to correct it. It was a simple error and everyone understood and forgave. But the senior judges, the commissaires, didn't agree. They, too, had seen what happened but the rules on the subject were very clear. They had no choice. The judge's decision, once given, is final. And Colignon had given his decision. The arguments lasted for more than two hours but in the end Hansen had to remain the champion of the world.

The British cycling papers dismissed it as yet more lunacy from lands which couldn't organise themselves as well as the British did. Michard had already put himself beyond the pale by having held a semi-professional contract earlier. But they lost interest long before the French press, which felt aggrieved for months, suggesting that the championship should be declared void, that future championships should be photographed . . . almost anything, really, if it would have given Michard his champion's jersey and medal. But despite the way the French dominated the UCI, the international body, they failed to declare Michard the winner. Instead, they opened a subscription to buy him a new jersey (an odd move, since a jersey costs so little) as a substitute for the champion's. Hansen, to his credit, didn't become world champion willingly and the two made quite a killing thereafter by staging revenge matches all over Europe.

6.

How to be eccentric

In one of the years when I lived in Belgium, the Tour de France started in Leiden, which is a town between The Hague and Amsterdam, not far from where fat sunbathing *frauleins* from the land of the economic miracle wobble with no clothes on.

All these places, of course, are in Holland and the fact that Holland is an entire nation away from the French shouldn't surprise you an atom when it comes to the Tour de France. Once, after all, it pedalled sullenly up and down the Plympton by-pass.

In fact, I was partly responsible for that. In the days when I worked at *Cycling*, I offered the editor a speculative piece on what it would be like if the Tour came here. It went everywhere else, so why not Britain? He told me it was the daftest idea he'd heard in a long while and I sulked and went home early. Later on, though, when I'd left *Cycling* and knew more of the ways of the world, I just wrote it anyway. I visualised sun-bronzed *coureurs* pedalling manfully up the A2 from Dover, their spokes sparkling, their strange foreign ways causing consternation in Canterbury. I had a wonderful time, and to my surprise it was published.

To my still greater surprise, the men from *L'Équipe* read it and took it as an official invitation. 'BRITANNIQUES WANT THE TOUR' was their headline. And there, in 1974, within two years, it had arrived. Not up the A2, admittedly, but on the Plympton by-pass, for the greater commercial glory of French artichoke farmers and the new ferry link to Roscoff. The farmers paid £180,000 for it, along with a couple of days on their own side. Plymouth, it was said, had put in rather less: £40,000.

I felt that strange, conceited swell of pride as *Cycling* spoke of this wonderful thing which would fill hotels and cram camp sites (none of which eventually happened). I followed developments of 'my' Tour de France in the *Daily Mirror*, which had some hand in events. With distinguished lack of self-aggrandisement I appointed myself to Plymouth, where I shook hands with Jacques Anquetil and made a phone call to Eddy Merckx, which he didn't answer. With a patronly smile, I watched two small boys try to unscrew the identity plates from the Molteni team car. I felt it served Eddy Merckx right. I turned to Johnny Hardcastle and told him how good I felt.

I had the inkling next day that things were not as I'd hoped. The massed ranks swept resentfully up and down the by-pass. There wasn't a breakaway all day. The grandstands weren't full. The sky was overcast. The race droned on and on for four hours and next day the *Daily Mirror* ran the headline: 'TOUR DE FRANCE: CAN 40 MILLION FRENCHMEN BE WRONG?'

On the way home, the riders were delayed at Exeter airport. It took days before everyone got back into their stride and I kept quiet about the whole thing for a long time.

The fabled publicity caravan drivers didn't bother crossing to Plymouth and spent the day in Roscoff instead, getting tiddly and playing *pétanque*. They did go to Leiden, though, and all the way up the motorway you could see grumpy Frenchmen driving lorries done up as dead flies and vacuum cleaners. The service stations were littered with half-inflated Michelin men looking for the gents'. Every time they passed each other, they shrugged in mutual sympathy at how ridiculous they looked.

It costs a lot of money to put a vehicle in the publicity troupe. The drivers don't see a thing of the race and by the end of the second stage they're getting hugely fed up with driving a dead fly round France at 22 mph, with the prospect of another month to come. At stage finishes, the publicity drivers are the ones with bad tempers, impending hangovers and very brown left arms, from leaning them out the window so much as they drive.

. . . Michelin men looking for the gents'.

I met Jacques Goddet at Leiden and feeling overawed at coming across him in the lift, I felt I ought to ask him a question. Jacques Goddet is a tall and imperial-looking man who, if he hadn't been organising the Tour de France since the day he took over from Henri Desgrange, would have looked well suited to running some colony somewhere. He's the next best thing France has got to De Gaulle and, as De Gaulle used to, he speaks grand, eloquent French from the era of the Sun King. He also likes wearing long shorts, long socks and a pith helmet when the sun shines, so that he looks locked into the Baden-Powell era. He used to run the Tour with his physical opposite, a sharp-eye, ferrety man with sunken cheeks and (you imagine, anyway) a natural feeling for Gauloises, berets and striped jerseys. To Goddet's De Gaulle, Félix Levitan would have played a good onion-seller. Goddet would have ruled the plantation like an absent-minded cultural attaché; Levitan looked right to run the penal colony.

'Ah, Monsieur Goddet,' I ventured, wondering if the lift would get to the bottom before I thought of what to say next. '*Je . . .*'

'*Et bien, Monsieur est anglais, je crois?*' he said. (Goddet has a soft spot for the English, having been educated at Oxford, although declining to speak English ever since.)

'*Oui, c'est vrai!*'. I knew I was gushing. My voice sounded remarkably like Joyce Grenfell's, but at least he understood that much. '*Est-ce que*, er, *vouz pouvez me dire combien*, er, it costs *pour organiser le Tour de France . . .*' (oh heck, is it *le* Tour or *la* Tour? Hell, push on . . . he'll understand) 'er, *s'il vous plaît?*'

I was writing for an American magazine and I could have done with the figure in dollars.

'I think,' he said after a while, 'it costs twelve and a half million francs.'

(Oh heck . . . two and a half francs to the guilder, one pound to four guilders, two and a bit dollars to the pound . . .)

The lift doors opened but my brain stayed shut.

'Old francs, of course,' Goddet added, and stepped out.

I met several bottles of wine and the man from the *Daily Express* on the next floor and he asked me what Goddet had said.

'That it costs twelve and a half million old francs to run the Tour de France,' I told him. And he said, 'Nonsense . . . here, take these and we'll go and get drunk. Bloody place; it's pouring out there.'

And it was. It was hammering down. Even the Dutch were getting worried. Much more and Holland could have filled up. The little boy with his finger in the dike might have been invented by an American story writer, but the ships from Harwich still have to approach slowly for fear their bow waves flood the place. You can imagine the bill Sealink would get for that.

Thighs and Back Wheel Ambrose had ideas of going to Holland once, to find fame and fortune in the criteriums. I think they had an interview in the local paper and they got as far as the travel agent's, but that was about the end of it.

As it happens, our town is twinned with a place in Holland and on his days off Thighs used to ride down to the local technical college to see whether there were any blue-eyed, country-breasted blonde Dutch girls there on an exchange visit. I think he still missed Amanda Lightbody, and rumours that she was coming back only made it worse. All he saw, though, was the Dutch mayor's wife and her daughter, who'd been carbo-loaded on cheese and milk for several years and bred to pull the plough. Her name was Marijke and Thighs said he could understand why Holland was so flat if it had her trampling it down all the time.

What we got instead, thanks to Back Wheel's contacts at the town hall, was the mayoress's son, a chap called Luuc, who had a square head and legs so thin and muscular that they looked like double-barrelled shotguns. Not that it ever slowed him down. We took him out training over hillier and hillier roads and he'd ride along whistling silly Dutch songs until we got so demoralised that we'd turn left while he wasn't looking and try to lose him.

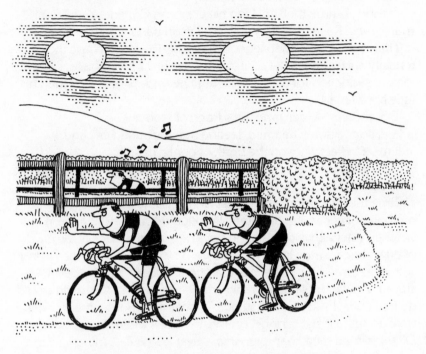

. . . we'd turn left while he wasn't looking . . .

He never got the hang of the Golden Crispycod 10-mile Challenge, though, and whenever Back Wheel tried to explain the romance of British time trialling, he'd scratch his cuboid Dutch noddle and say 'Zo, you must ride all ze way zare and zen you are coming all ze way back again, jus' to see who is coming zare and back again faster zan ze uzzers? It is unreal, *ja?*'

Put like that, we had to agree it was, and Aubrey Fothergill, who considered that all Englishmen had won first prize in the lottery of life, marked us down as subversives.

'Big thing to us, time trialling,' Aubrey barked at Luuc one day, oozing conviction and nostalgia, thumbs behind braces and double chin protruding like the rim of a bumper car. 'You Continentals, y'call it t'Race of Truth, eh lad? Not surprised, really.'

Luuc looked puzzled.

'Sorry?'

'Race of Truth, lad . . . time trialling,' said Aubrey in the way of the English dealing with foreigners, repeating the same words more stressfully but without the verbs.

'Race of trooce?' Luuc tried to say.

'Aye lad . . . time trialling. Don't like 'em on Continent, eh? Real man's race. Race of Truth y'call 'em in yon parts, don't yer?'

This is good bike shop legend, that only the British have the tenacity and pureness of soul to ride The Test of Manliness. Luuc looked saddened for a little while until he understood. And then his face brightened.

'Oh, you say we call time trials Race of Trooce?'

'Aye, son.' Aubrey beamed, feeling that his prejudices and lifetime's beliefs were on the brink of confirmation.

'No,' said Luuc very thoughtfully, 'I don't zink I have ever heard zem called zat.'

Time trialling, is indeed, a great British tradition. It also follows our habit of accepting disasters, like Dunkirk, and calling them victories. After all, we only started riding against the clock at the crack of dawn because we lost the battle for open, publicised road racing.

It soon turned out to be less than perfect logic, but the belief stayed that we Brits had it cracked if only the rest of the world would do it our way. In 1912, for instance, it looked as though the Swedes were about to insist on lone, unassisted rides when they ran the Olympic road race championship – over 200 miles, mind – round Lake Malar.

'Unpaced,' said the editor of *Cycling*, 'we do not think that any nation possesses a rider equal to Moss or Grubb.'

The Swedes, though, changed their mind at the last moment. Riders would start at intervals, but they could pace anyone they caught or who could catch them. This was a formula guaranteed to confuse – not only in the race but afterwards. One of the English team said he felt too uncertain in a bunch and insisted on riding at the front. In complaining that the Americans in the group wouldn't come by and share the pacemaking, though, he overlooked the fact that he'd preferred that they didn't. And so it went on.

What made it even less wise to complain was that the winner, G.R.

It sounds absurd now, but around the turn of the century there was a paced tricycle race on the Great North Road, which could then have been little more than a country lane. Anyway, these paced tricyclists alarmed a horsewoman, who complained to the chief constable of Huntingdonshire, who then banned all cycle racing in the county.

The National Cyclists' Union went further and banned racing of any sort on the road. A separate organisation began for time trialling, leading to the present-day split of jurisdiction between the British Cycling Federation and the RTTC.

The RTTC, with the best of motives, sought to avoid notice by dressing all riders in 'inconspicuous' black and starting races in secret, early on Sundays and miles from anywhere. The original wise quest for secrecy soon became an obsession, to the extent that the national champion, Ralph Dougherty, was disqualified for wearing light-coloured socks in a '25' during 1944. The fact that the roads were empty and the world at war didn't matter; secrecy was to be preserved.

Lewis, the one South African, had started in the first three, passed the others early on and ridden all but the first few miles alone. It limited the consolation that Freddie Grubb did indeed come second, and his team-mate Leon Meredith fourth.

Still, the view that we would overcome was proved correct in 1922 when we did the promotion job ourselves in the world championships and changed the formula to the way that suited us best – a true solo time trial. Dave Marsh won and we collected all three medals. The Continentals then took back the promotion and returned to the original formula.

In 1931, the Danes for some reason decided to go back to the solo style. This was great excitement for the British. We named our team as Freddy Frost, F.T. Brown (reserve), Len Cave and Frank Southhall.

'Loiterer' enthused in *Cycling*: 'We are promised good roads this year . . . and our men are fitter than ever. It is, therefore . . . perfectly easy to jot down the English times, note the best times abroad over

the distance, and announce the result of the race long before the
starter has given the Danish equivalent for the word "go"!'

Then, although the headline read 'If perfectly fit, Southall will win',
came a note of caution, although for none of the reasons that
eventually transpired.

'I cannot tell you who is going to win,' Loiterer warned. 'Theory
and practice do not seem to line up in international events.'

He was right. A week later, it was the editor himself saying: 'The
placings . . . give the English riders lowly positions. It may appear
ungracious, but we do not accept this as a true indication of their
relative merits. There is no pleasure to us in wrangling or holding an
"inquest" on races which we have lost, but we are disappointed that
such a clear-headed nation as the Danes should not have given a
little deeper thought to the requirements . . .'

Two things had happened. The first was that the police, realising
that riders would be alone and therefore needing less room or
protection, decided against closing the roads. The second was that
the Danish organisers, not realising what would happen, didn't stop
anyone who fancied from following their favourites. Therefore, what
the English had imagined would be a British-style race of strictly
solo racing, ended up in much the manner of small boys riding
behind corporation buses. As 'Our Special Correspondent' began
his report: 'Henry Hansen, of Denmark, and a convoy of motorcars
around him for the majority of the last forty-six miles, won the
amateur road championship of the world . . .

'It is equally serious and equally true to say that the whole race
was as badly organised as a road time trial could be and was a
disgrace . . .'

The benefits of riding behind another rider are colossal – and the
last forty-six of the 107 miles from Copenhagen to Baarse and back
were into a gale. Unpaced riders wouldn't have reached 20 mph.

Hansen shared the going with Olmo of Italy, and also tacked on
behind Southall. Southall, seeing the way things were going, took
pace for the last 20 miles from the town of Koge onwards. That was
where Hansen and cortège caught him.

'When in Denmark, do as the Danes do,' he said afterwards.

What made the race still more fun was that the timekeeper often
couldn't see the finishing line because of all the journalists
crowding round him for the very times that he was supposed to be
taking. Nor could he hear the official who checked the riders'

numbers, so that the information reached him via the journalists after being translated and re-translated on the way.

Sometimes, as when Southall crossed the line, there was too much confusion to write down the whole time. Southall, timed by one of the British contingent in 5:6:26, had his seconds missed off and went down as 5:6. At least five riders got the wrong times and even when the judges met afterwards to sort out the mess, it was still anybody's guess who'd done precisely what. Southall's time was readjusted to 5:6:30, the extra half minute looking no more than a guess.

At one moment, the timekeeper logged in number 60 (Olmo), even though reporters said it was number 53 (Wanzenried of Switzerland). Three-quarters of an hour later, the Italians arrived to protest, stopping the timekeeper doing his job altogether. By then all the journalists were joining in, too, arguing or disputing that Olmo had crossed the line 'one second after Harry Hansen'. In the end, number 53's time, previously recorded by number 60's name, was transferred to number 66. Olmo therefore became second in the amateur championship of the world and Wanzenried isn't in the result sheet at all.

7.

How to be very French indeed

As I was saying, everyone got to Leiden, Jacques Goddet got out of the lift and the man from the *Daily Express* said it was raining.* It was raining so hard, in fact, that the people from *L'Équipe* got terribly alarmed and said they weren't going to hold the prologue

---

By odd coincidence, I once met Joop Zoetemelk – who comes from Leiden but lives in France – in exactly the same circumstances. There used to be a very long race from London to Holyhead which then became Bristol–Bradford before it finally disappeared altogether.

This race from Bristol started at some impossible time and so it was that I met Joop Zoetemelk in the hotel lift at 4 am. He wasn't having much of a season and he wasn't at all cheerful about riding miles and miles past endless branches of Top Shop and the Halifax Building Society just to get to Bradford, of which he'd heard little and liked even less.

'I'm afraid it's raining, Mr Zoetemelk,' I told him. It didn't cheer him up a bit. In fact, he didn't even believe me.

'De meneer zegt dat het regent . . .' he told a hanger-on: 'go and have a look for yourself'.

The erk went and had a look and came back and told Zoetemelk it was raining. It cheered me up no end.

time trial after all because the roads were cobbled and slimy and everyone would fall off.

'We are all agreed about this,' said the communiqué.

Well, it was bunkum. They didn't agree at all. So what they decided to do was hold the time trial after all but say it didn't count. The race went ahead, the Dutch did extraordinarily well (since it was only to them that it was important) and the rain continued to pour. Eventually the crowd got wind of what was going on, word spread to the town hall, and the big cheeses of the municipality sued the Tour de France for the £50,000 they'd paid to get the race there in the first place.

It was altogether an odd Tour because one of the main backers was in gaol, the Dutch organiser was in hospital, a prominent Dutch rider was ticked off for larking about, the Belgian national champion was thrown out, and an American started but didn't finish.

The Dutchman was a smooth-faced chap called Gerben Karstens. His greatest triumph was to stop during the previous year's Tour and lie on the ground with his bike in the air above him.

... lie on the ground with his bike in the air ...

Photographers rushed to take the picture, Karstens hopped back on and got back to the race, and one of the pictures later won a big award for sports photography.

The American was a straight-laced Californian called Jonathon Boyer, although the Press called him Jacques and the Americans named him Jock. He was a pleasant enough chap and we spent a happy week together when he stayed in Belgium during his time with the Lejeune team. There aren't many English speakers on the Tour, even now, and then there were fewer still. Thinking Jonathon/ Jacques/Jock might have run out of light entertainment by mid-distance, a British reporter asked him if he'd like a paperback.

'Thank you, but no,' said Boyer with characteristic earnestness. 'I have my Bible.'

There's nothing, of course, wrong or even strange about this; it's just that for a bike rider, it's fairly unusual. Bike riders aren't accustomed to thinking of Sundays as a day of rest, after all. But in fact Boyer was in good American lineage. Major Taylor, the phenomenal sprinter at the turn of the century, missed several chances to defend or acquire his world sprint championship because the races were held on a Sunday. Just as Larry Hagman (J.R. in *Dallas*) has a personal rule never to speak on Sunday, so Taylor wouldn't race on one.

Anyway, to get back to Boyer and his Bible for a moment, he probably needed it four years later, if only to swear on. Boyer was climbing the final hill at Goodwood, 500 yards from becoming world champion and seconds clear of the field. Until then he hadn't won a real professional race, his only victory having been in the south of France early one season when, in a splendid episode reminiscent of the Bessums 'Best for Radiators' End-of-Season Grand Prix, everybody but Boyer went the wrong way. Fading fast but dragged on by the exhilaration that only a rainbow jersey can provide, he was suddenly passed by his team-mate, Greg LeMond. The two are far from friends.

Not only did LeMond pass him but he brought Beppe Saronni and Sean Kelly with him as well. The Italian, knowing that he was sure of at least silver if he did nothing, but risking everything if he took everyone else up to Boyer, waited to see what would happen. If you look at pictures taken at that moment, you can see him smiling as LeMond took the initiative and bridged the gap.

Saronni won, LeMond was second and Kelly third. Boyer, who'd been fifth at Sallanches behind Bernard Hinault, finished several places back. I doubt if LeMond and Boyer have exchanged more than a few words since. I went to see Boyer afterwards. I asked for a few considered words and got the impression that he was very cross indeed. He lives in Italy these days.

At the finish, sitting in the press room, I was first to get to Kelly. Normally, of course, he speaks French or Flemish (he lived at Vilvoorde, near Brussels), but today he was in England. We spoke English. Or at least, I did. Kelly's English is at the same time high-pitched, staccato, very Irish and with a French intonation. He 'makes' everything. He makes an interview, makes a good ride, makes a success. And every sentence ends with a kind of high, questioning 'oop?' sound.

'I make a very good race, *oop?* But Saronni, he makes an attack, *oop?* But I'm very happy, *oop*, and Greg, he makes a good sprint, *oop?*'

After just such an interview in Prague, for the Irish radio station RTE, I played the interview back to fellow English-speaking reporters in the press room and over a few beers we held a sweepstake on what we thought Kelly might have said. RTE later said that they couldn't take an interview played over the phone lines because of a union problem, but they'd listen to it anyway. I told the man in Dublin about the sweepstake and, having heard Kelly crackling over from Czechoslovakia, he said he'd like to buy a ticket.

'Sure I don't know what the boy says,' he laughed, 'but I'll buy a ticket anyway.'

In wonderful Irish style, Sean Kelly's name isn't Sean at all. He was named in fact after his father, whose name is John. Hence his real name is John Kelly. But having done that, the family realised the confusion it would cause, having two Johns in the same household. So ever since they've called him Sean.

Anyway, after several minutes of making this and that in English, the considerable and considerably gesticulating French contingent realised they were missing the story.

'*Parlez français!*' they insisted, and Sean politely asked them to *attendez*, and they had to wait, which for we English was the next best thing to winning a medal. With the help of an Irishman, we'd put one over on the French. The Irish might dwell on the Easter Uprising but for us that day in the press hall it was like an action replay of the Battle of Agincourt.

The French press corps is an odd bunch. The French are more predictable than the Italians, who swing alarmingly between ecstatic and suicidal according to the result, and better fun than the Spanish, who are always gloomy and come down last for breakfast, talking only to each other.

The head man of the French contingent is a spreading maestro called Pierre Chany, who, for *L'Équipe*, writes endless sentences of bewildering, *grande époque* complexity. They remind you of the way someone once criticised the American news magazine, *Time*: 'Backward run the sentences until giddy reels the mind.'

The *L'Équipe* style is to begin a 5,000-word report with a discussion of the weather, move on through the emotions, the culture, the gastronomy of the region and its greatest philosophers, and only then report that: '. . . five riders were seriously injured, the world champion ended his career with hepatitis, and the race was abandoned.' *L'Équipe* has never been strong on the Mark Twain parody of putting all the important facts up front: 'Dead – that's what he was when he hit the bar-room floor.' Nor does it see much virtue in the *Sun's* policy of avoiding words of more than three syllables.

Chany, ever imperious, was so upset with the progress of the world championship at Heerlen in Holland, when Francesco Moser and Gerrie Knetemann were away alone and no Frenchman was in sight, that he pointedly turned his back on the press room televisions and got on with something else instead.

Chany and the whole staff of *L'Équipe* are the inheritors of old man Desgrange himself and the flower-power school of prose writing.

'There are four of them,' Desgrange once wrote of riders in Paris–Brest–Paris. 'Their legs, like giant levers, will power onwards for sixty hours; their muscles will grind up the kilometres; their broad chests will heave with the effort of the struggle; their hands will clench the handlebars; with their eyes they will observe each other ferociously; their backs will bend forward in unison for barbaric breakaways; their stomachs will fight against hunger, their brains against sleep.

'And at night a peasant waiting for them by a deserted road will see four demons passing by . . .'

Of his first Tour de France, he forecast: 'From Marseille to Bordeaux, passing along the roseate and dreaming roads sleeping under the sun, across the calm of the fields of the Vendée, following the Loire which flows on still and silent, our men are going to race madly, unflaggingly.'

Which was all cracking good stuff, and certainly a lot better than what the local paper made of the Bessums 'Best for Radiators' End-of-Season Grand Prix fiasco. I suppose Desgrange was a contemporary of old Bidlake's, and equally dubious about women. For many years women were barred from following the Tour de France – something to do, it was said, with gentleman racers relieving themselves as they rode – although before the ban was lifted an American journalist did manage to smuggle herself into the entourage by disguising herself as a bloke. Desgrange saw himself as a guiding light in matters of training and his articles pointed riders on the path of chastity. A serious rider, he said, 'would have no more need of a woman than of his first pair of socks'.

For all that Desgrange achieved, I find it hard to see the pursuit of chastity among racing cyclists as a subject in which he succeeded. Remember that when they found old Leonardo da Vinci's sketch of the first bicycle, it was tucked in among a heap of

---

Desgrange trained first not as a journalist but as a solicitor's clerk. Quaintly, his habit of riding to work with bare calves upset his employers, who insisted he either wear socks or leave. Desgrange, who clearly had a thing about socks, chose to go.

I don't know what he would have been like as a solicitor, but he made a pretty good racing cyclist, setting the first world record for the unpaced hour: 35.325 km. After that, he became a cantankerous old man. When he guaranteed Major Taylor $7,500 in a match against the French favourite, Edmond Jacquelin, Desgrange naturally hoped the Frenchman would win. When, instead, he lost, he contemptuously paid Taylor his $7,500 – a vast sum at the start of the century – in ten-centime pieces.

pornographic sketches. And Desgrange's appeal for sexual innocence can hardly take credit for Thighs Sweeting's triumphs in the Golden Crispycod 10-mile Challenge, since chastity in Sweeting's case is something imposed not by willpower but by his own incompetence, urged along by the several layers of anoraks and woollies that surrounded the person of Amanda Lightbody.

Thighs was always very secretive about his successes with Amanda, as indeed it's always easy to remain silent about something that doesn't exist. But almost unexpectedly, the whole issue raised itself once again. It was a spring Wednesday evening that the rumours proved true: she had come back from Africa, quite unwilling to talk about what had happened there, but somehow changed. Predictably, it was Johnny Hardcastle who found out first, having stopped to help the schoolboy champion distribute the week's free newspapers and therefore riding uncustomarily past Amanda's house. He spread the news the following night and Thighs went straight round after an evening '25' with two new tubulars as a 'welcome home' present and as many copies as he could find of all the *Cycling*s she'd missed while she'd been away. He'd been afraid that the crewcut youth from the Fenland Clarion might already be round there with more free ice lollies and his feet already under the table, but of him there was no sign.

Thighs was his usual pitiable sight, standing on the doorstep in an aura of embrocation, shuffling from one foot to the other and quite oblivious to the hissing of a slowly deflating front tubular. Later he'd have to push the bike up the road and round the corner before he mended it, aware that Mandy might find a slow puncture somehow unmanly.

When she answered the door, she was dressed in frayed jeans and a pale blue blouse with no sleeves. She had bare feet. The sight of her so lightly dressed, her skin still golden from the African sun, made all the little hormones jump up and down inside him. He could feel them all tickling the inside of his stomach. He said later that it was exactly the feeling he got at the start of the Hemel Hempstead hilly time trial (where, incidentally, he'd been caught for two minutes by Dutch Luuc and had gone home in a dreadful sulk).

With a shy little smile, he handed over his armfuls of presents.

'Thank you,' Amanda said, her spine bent from several months of BBAR details, equipment reviews and paranoid letters from people in Surrey. But she didn't ask him in. When we asked at the clubroom what had happened, he said she'd been out. He hadn't been able to ask her out after all. Johnny Hardcastle knew better. He said that Thighs had given up hope of getting Amanda to the mud-wrestling in Leicester and had been thinking instead of a new night-club on the Nuneaton ring-road.

Going to night-clubs can be good for a chap. In 1933, Georges Speicher won the Tour de France. The French feder-ation then assumed that so massive an effort would make him too tired to ride the world championship, to be held at Montlhéry and where, incidentally, spectators were to be charged for the first time. This disappointed Speicher but he shrugged and decided to give himself a holiday instead. He was, as it happened, a great fan of cabarets and music halls and, particularly, of Maurice Chevalier. There, in the halls, 'Gorgeous George' could act the part of a dandy. And so he left for Paris.

At the last moment, however, the French changed their mind. Georges Choque had fallen ill and Speicher was wanted as reserve. A search party was sent to scour the night life of the capital and Speicher was eventually found at three o'clock, on the morning of the race.

A professional for little more than a year, he rode the world championship and won by five minutes, the first time any rider had won the Tour and the arc-en-ciel *in the same season.*

Next day he resumed his tour of the night-clubs.

But to get back to the French for a moment, most of the recent heroes of the Tour are still with us. History has recorded the winners of the old Tours but not a lot about them. There are the legends that live on, of course, like the little Frenchman Eugène Christophe, '*Cri-Cri, le vieux Gaulois*', who broke his forks on the descent of the Tourmalet in 1913.

Eugène Christophe is now best known for the make of toeclips that carry his name. But his is a remarkable story. Years afterwards he recalled:

'All of a sudden, about ten kilometres from St Marie de Campan

down in the valley, I felt that something is wrong with my handlebar.
I cannot steer my bike any more. I pull on my brakes and stop. I see
my fork is broken! I can tell you now that my fork was broken, but I
would not tell you at that time because it was bad advertising for my
firm.

'So there I was, left alone on the road. When I say the road, I
should say the path. I thought that maybe one of these steep pack
trails would lead me straight to St Marie de Campan. But I was
crying so badly I couldn't see anything. With my bike on my
shoulder, I walked for all those ten kilometres.

'On arriving in the village I met a young girl who led me to the
blacksmith on the other side of the village. M. Lecomte was the
name of the blacksmith. He was a nice man and he wanted to help
me, but he wasn't allowed to. The regulations were strict. I had to do
all the repair myself. I never spent a more wretched time in my life
than these cruel hours in M. Lecomte's forge.

'Members of rival cycling firms had been sent to keep a close
watch on me. M. Lecomte was only allowed to give me verbal
guidance. A young boy helped me handling the bellows, for which
aid I was fined. After three hours' repair I was able to continue on an
uncertain and rather unsafe bike. I had lost the Tour de France.'

It seems pretty rotten luck nowadays, especially when you see
riders hanging on to the team cars while they have their shoeplates
re-tightened, or their teeth brushed, or (as was once said of Greg
LeMond) to make quick radiophone calls to his stockbroker.

There's a memorial now where that remarkable incident took
place and I've always wanted to find it. When that true gentleman,
Jock Wadley, was editor of *Sporting Cyclist*, he managed to be
there when Christophe re-enacted the incident, by then an old and
stooped man.

Astonishingly, history was to repeat itself. Christophe survived the
First World War and was leading the 1919 Tour de France in the last
but one stage, some 468 kilometres from Metz to Dunkirk. He was
wearing the very first *maillot jaune*, the yellow jersey which
Desgrange had used at the suggestion of a journalist called
Alphonse Bauge to pick out the winner and further advertise his
paper, which he printed on yellow paper.

Sure enough, on roads still unrepaired from the war, Christophe's
fork broke. The village and its forge was only a mile away, but he
was held up for two hours and dropped from first to tenth, or last

A young boy helped me handling the bellows . . .

but one, because the rest of the field had dropped out. He still holds the record for the greatest time span between victories – 1906 to 1925 – and he's unlikely to lose it.

Christophe now, like Jock Wadley, is no longer with us. Both, in their very different ways, were legends.

8.

How to succumb to gravity

Moving away to the new marital home proved a turning point for Back Wheel Ambrose. He was working at the town hall, which until the move had been only three minutes' walk away. Cycling such a short distance would hardly have been worth the problem of putting a shine on his suit trousers. It was doubtful that Sylvie would have let him, anyway, because she'd become terribly houseproud and saw the way she turned Back Wheel out in the morning as a reflection on her abilities as a housewife.

On the other hand, I once worked at a newspaper in Hertfordshire where so many people were keen cyclists – the editor, the ad manager, a sports reporter and me – that nobody could get into the gents' in the morning for half-naked and knackered men washing and changing their shirts. The only way to the editorial office was through a stream of soapy, steaming water which inched under the door and across the corridor floor.

We swapped French cycling magazines in the way other men exchange *Mayfair*. Johnny Hardcastle, who is a year or more on from the rest of us, belongs to the era when men were men and clubrooms were full of disintegrating copies of *Mirroir de Cyclisme*. He says they were wonderful days, sipping cocoa while the mist settled on their leather saddles outside.

In Johnny Hardcastle's day, that was the only way you knew what was happening beyond Kent. The magazines were full of men covered in blood and grimacing excitedly after a *chute terrible*.

They were always suffering *chutes terribles*, which seemed much more romantic than any encounter we might suffer with the baker's van. For years I believed Continental racing cyclists had more blood than the rest of us. When I fell off, I got a scab. When they came off, there was blood everywhere. If they'd had mothers like Mrs Hardcastle they'd have got more stick over it than it was worth, bringing home blood-soaked jerseys like that. Later on, someone took me to one side and suggested that all these distant heroes were without doubt doped to the eyebrows, and it was that and not a sense of theatrical duty which was making their arteries work overtime.

The magazines were also full of Frenchmen with goggles strapped round their upper arms. I think that must have lasted into the 1950s – well into the 1950s, come to think of it – because Johnny Hardcastle once admitted to having a pair of goggles of his own somewhere, and that he'd bought them to look more like Louison Bobet.

These days, of course, nobody knows who Louison Bobet is. He was the 1954 world champion, in fact, and the last of an era when men rode with spare tyres looped over their shoulders. It is my theory that he has been forgotten because the younger and therefore smaller a club member was, the less likely he was to be allowed to read the magazines. Schoolboy champions in those days knew their place and didn't turn up with bikes that the rest of us couldn't afford.

Anyway, to get back to riding to work. Later, I was regarded with suspicion because, by contrast, I was the *only* bikie in the place. I'd turn up each morning dressed in a mixture of crown jester and parakeet and they, of course, would smirk. Over the months, though, they figured out what I was saving on petrol and bus fares and, since I didn't smoke or drink, and hadn't got the energy to do anything else after twenty-five miles each way across the Fens, I was popularly regarded to be rolling in it. One by one other employees started riding to work, and within the year the management felt obliged to build new bike sheds.

But back to Sylvie Ambrose for a moment. She'd set her heart on one of the two-bedroomed executive *pied-à-terres* with dream kitchen, avocado bathroom fittings and carport that were going up on the edge of town, complete with fitted wardrobes and door chime.

Until the builders got it, we'd always known the land as Cemetery End, and the 30 mph signs alongside it were the finishing point for the Wednesday-night burn-ups. No sooner had the 'Land Acquired' signs gone up, though, than Cemetery End became The Cuckoo-pints. It became populated over several months by the kind of people – apart from Sylvie, Ambrose and the children (Jason, 18 months and Tracy-Dianne, 2 months) – who buy leatherette-tooled books of Dickens from the Sunday newspaper magazines and itch to varnish the lamp post at the end of their garden.

No one in The Cuckoopints was happier than Sylvie, who found that a nice class of neighbour was a great consolation for the kind of friends that Back Wheel kept bringing home. Sylvie was very proud that the man across the road was a doctor. It brought tone to the estate, she said. Back Wheel told everybody the neighbour was a trainee gynaecologist and insisted that he'd seen him trying to decorate the hall with his arm through the letter box.

Over the years, we came to realise just how dull Sylvie was. After the Open 100, where Sylvie was helping push off, Aubrey Fothergill wrote in the club newsletter that she'd been 'the rock around which everything at the start revolved'. Unfortunately a slip of the typewriter rendered the word as 'roc'. In some ways it was more accurate than ever since, as Johnny Hardcastle's mother pointed out during a family game of Scrabble, the dictionary defines 'roc' as 'a fabulous bird of immense size and strength', which just about summed Sylvie up.

It became a joke which Sylvie never got to understand. Wit wasn't her strongest point. Nor was sheer intelligence. When the club dinner came round, Thighs said during his speech that Sylvie had once been asked for the most impressive invention in the world. Sylvie, according to the story, had thought for a while and then answered 'the Thermos flask'.

Astounded, her questioner asked why the vacuum flask when the wheel, the micro-chip and the employment of electricity had brought so much of benefit to the world.

'So Sylvie thought for a while,' Thighs said, 'and then she answered: "I'll tell you why . . ."'

He paused for dramatic effect and sipped his orange juice.

'"Because," said Sylvie, "you can put cold things in a Thermos flask and it'll keep them cold. And you can put hot things in and it'll keep them hot."

'"Yes," said the questioner, "yes, so what?"'

'"Well," said Sylvie, very impressed, "but how does it *know*?"'

Everybody laughed and Amanda Lightbody looked delightedly up at Thighs, who, at last, had persuaded her to join him.

Poor Sylvie was so myopic that apart from occasional excursions on the tandem, she never managed to ride a bike very much. There'd been great speculation at the committee meeting whether she should be allowed to do the pushing-off at the '100' at all. It wasn't a question of whether she had the strength. Of that there was no doubt. And several years of enthusiastic child raising had given her the bulk as well. It was more a question of whether she'd see far enough to push the riders in the right direction.

After considerable discussion, Johnny Hardcastle said she'd get the hang of it by about number 15 and that if, after half an hour, she still showed any sign of rocking riders forwards rather than backwards on the count of 'five', he'd take over himself. And so it was agreed.

'Sylvie Ambrose was the roc around which everything at the start revolved,' said Aubrey in the magazine afterwards. 'There were some nervous moments at first but she soon became the master, or should I say mistress, of all she was asked.'

The truth is that the despondency in the first rider's eyes will haunt me for many seasons. He was only a youngish chap, for all I know having his first ride at the distance. Usually we put our own rider off first, which is the tradition, but this year we had no riders, and so it had to be someone else.

'Ten!' shouted the timekeeper.

Number 1 reached for a final tug at his toestraps.

'Five!'

Sylvie got the rocking motion started and number 1 took two theatrical deep breaths and a tighter grasp of his handlebars. His nerves started a little tic in his left eye.

'Four,' the timekeeper shouted. The rocking increased.

'Three.'

For a moment, the tic besides, number 1's face was a mask of concentration. It was impressive to see. But slowly it dawned on him that Sylvie was rolling him forwards and not backwards. You could see him doing the calculation, his eyeballs swivelling slightly as he counted off the remaining seconds in his head. And then, with that feeling of unstoppable inevitability, he came to the awful and very real conclusion that he was going to be pushed backwards and not forwards on the word 'go'.

'Two!'

'No, no,' he started to shout, now panicking. The timekeeper looked up, taken aback by this bizarre behaviour.

'Wrong way, wrong way!', number 1 shouted. The tic was much worse, I noticed.

Sylvie had come to the end of her backwards rock and was putting him back into forward motion.

'Stop, stop!' the rider shouted again, begging her, imploring her in the fraction of seconds he had left. But by then it was too late. He was already going forwards again.

Suddenly the timekeeper realised he was no longer looking at his watch and cast his eyes quickly down again. It was just as well. Sylvie, registering something was wrong, tensed her not inconsiderable muscles and began rolling her rider back the other way. Number 1 gave up concentrating on the start and started trying to fend off Sylvie instead. That, if anything, was his final undoing.

'Go!'

At 7:01 on a Sunday morning in July, neither Sylvie, number 1, nor the timekeeper, nor the man from *Cycling*, knew what was going on. It was a sorrowful sight. As the final instruction came, Sylvie just let go. It was the only solution she could think of in the time. Number 1 was still flailing wildly at Sylvie with his arm and, by now unsupported, he toppled slowly to the verge with a thud.

Two crows flapped away from a nearby tree.

'Number 2!' shouted the timekeeper with considerable presence of mind as rider and bicycle rotated gently through ninety degrees to fall at his feet. He jumped from his fisherman's stool to avoid him.

'Stupid *** fool,' number 1 swore, by now on the ground and still trapped in the wreckage of his bike.

'Number 2!' yelled the timekeeper again, hurriedly restarting the watch which he'd stopped while jumping out of the way.

'Stupid *** *** fool,' number 1 hollared once more. 'Stupid *** *** *** fool.' Sylvie burst into tears.

'Morning number two,' said the timekeeper, now having lost interest in the eleven stones of skinsuit at his feet. 'I think number 1's technically having a late start.'

Crashes, inevitably, are all part of balancing on two wheels. Sometimes they're pretty minor, sometimes (as when Back Wheel Ambrose predictably fells the entire bunch in the last 200 metres of

In modern Tours de France, riders don't need pushers-off at all. They race down ramps out the back of hired bread vans. I've never met anyone who could explain why this was either desirable or necessary, and I can only assume that it's some kind of Common Market regulation that we never quite grasped.

the opening race of the season) they're just plain miserable. And sometimes they're so spectacular that they pass into history. In 1960, for example, Roger Rivière had already won three stages of the Tour de France when he hurtled off the edge of the Col de Perjuret. It was just his second Tour and he'd been predicting a win. Instead he so badly injured himself that he never raced again – the sad loss of a huge talent.

They took Rivière to hospital by road and there was much speculation later that, had they used the helicopters now so common on the race, the change in air pressure might have killed him.

Just as spectacular but much happier was the incredible tumble that the very barrel-shaped Dutchman, Wim van Est, suffered on the Col d'Aubisque in 1951, on the day that he wore Holland's first *maillot jaune*. In the autumn of 1989 he entertained me with the story.

'The day before, I was away with a group of thirteen, fourteen riders. And there was a really fast rider with us, Caput, the Frenchman. Good sprinter. He attacked a kilometre from the line but we got him back. But when we got to the track, it was an ash track, a horse-racing track.

'Well, on a track like that, I was unbeatable. I'd raced on those sort of finishes so often . . . Coppi, Kubler . . . that I was unbeatable. And I won and I took the yellow jersey.

'Next day there were several cols. The Tourmalet was one, and then the Aubisque. There were nine or ten men away and we were gritting our teeth to get them back, and then in the first bend of the descent, there was just Ockers and Coppi, a few hundred metres in front of us.

'That first bend, it was wet, slippery from the snow. And there were sharp stones on the road that the cars had kicked up and my front wheel hit them and I went over.

'Well, there was a drop of twenty metres. They've built a barrier round it now, but then there was nothing to stop you going over. I fell twenty metres, rolling and rolling and rolling. My feet had come out of the straps, my bike had disappeared, and I curled myself up in a ball and I rolled and rolled.

'And twenty metres down this drop, there was a little flat area, the only one that's there, no bigger than the seat of a chair, and suddenly I hit it and I landed on my backside. A metre left or right and I'd have dropped on to solid stone, six or seven hundred metres down.

'My ankles were all hurt, my elbows were all *kapot*, I was all bruised and shaken up, and I didn't know where I was, but nothing was broken.

'I just lay there. And the other riders were going by, I could see, and then right up at the top I could make out my team-mate, Gerrit Peeters, looking down at me.

'"You looked just like a buttercup down there," he said to me afterwards. "With the yellow jersey on, you know."'

Half the field didn't realise what had happened and they were still hurtling after van Est, mile after mile, so that they still hadn't seen him by the time they got to the finish. The bloke who won the stage thought he'd come second and was presumably quite mystified to find no sign of van Est.

Back up on the mountain, the Dutch team car stopped, along with others, on the top of the Aubisque. They tried throwing a towing rope over to him, but it was far too short. Pulling it back up again, they lengthened it with the only things they could find . . .

'They got forty tubulars, knotted them together, tied them to the tow rope, and threw it down to me. It was all the tubs that our manager, Kees Pellenaars, had for the team. By the time they'd tugged me up, all the tubs were stretched and they wouldn't stay on the wheels any more! Forty tubs!

'I wanted to get on my bike and start riding again. One of the journalists gave me a flask of cognac, and I was saying 'I want to go on, I want to go on!' But I couldn't. The whole team, Pellenaars stopped the whole team.

'"We'll be back next year," he said. It was good publicity. I got home and the whole neighbourhood was out to greet me! *Ja, hoor* . . . those were crazy days.'

Johnny Hardcastle owns a wonderful book called *The Art &*

. . . knotted them together, tied them to the tow rope . . .

Pastime of Cycling, which he lent to me once. It came out in Ireland at the end of last century and contains advice which Wim van Est would have been wise to heed.

'A day may come when your machine seems to get beyond your control,' it says, 'and fairly run away with you. In such a case, if you see that the hill is not very steep, and the bottom is in view, or if you are acquainted with it and know that it is possible to descend, then stick to your saddle, keep cool, and steer a straight course . . .

'If, however, you wait too long, and the machine is running at, say, sixteen or eighteen miles an hour, and going quicker each moment, and you feel that the hill is dangerous, you must not, no matter what the cost, stick to the saddle . . .

'If you find you are unable to dismount owing to the pace, and steepness of the gradient, go for the nearest hedge or hawthorn bush, and, just as you approach, throw your legs over the handles. You are sure to be hurt, but you may escape with only a few scrapes and bruises, whereas to hold on means more or less injury.

'If no hedge or hawthorn bush is near, throw your legs over the handles and put the brake hard on, and you will shoot forward and alight on your feet, when you must make every effort to keep on your feet and run as hard as you can, for your bicycle is in eager pursuit, and a stroke from it may place you *hors de combat*.

'The man who is dependent on his brake, and never back-pedals, is helpless should his brake go wrong. Every rider should practise the art, and thus prepare himself for any emergency.'

. . . go for the nearest hedge or hawthorn bush . . .

There . . . what would van Est have given to have known that, up there on the Col d'Aubisque?

The Aubisque plays another important role in Tour history. Henri Desgrange not only introduced the Pyrénées in 1910 but he did it on a stage of no less than 330 km, from Luchon to Bayonne. Now, the Pyrénées these days are run through by first-class roads and hold quite sizeable towns. Then, though, they were a wilderness known only by sheep and shepherds. The roads were merely tracks and there was doubt whether riders would even find their way across.

Desgrange, delighted at this new twist in his race, drove to the summit of the Aubisque, at 5,610 feet, and waited along with his officials for his riders to pass.

They waited and waited. They waited so long that they feared the competitors had given up, or fallen, like van Est, into the ravine. Finally a rider struggled painfully slowly towards them, on foot, his head slumped. He couldn't speak and passed in exhausted, sullen silence.

Another quarter of an hour passed before the eventual winner, Octave Lapize, came the same way.

'Où sont les autres?' cried Desgrange. 'Where are the rest?'

Lapize didn't answer immediately. Instead, he stared at Desgrange with pain-ridden eyes and only then hissed the one word: 'Murderers!'

Not that all the crashes were actually that accidental.

'We never had any money, so you had to be clever,' said van Est. 'We used to have a trick to get a drink while we were out training. We'd get to a shop and then one of us would fall off and lie in the kerb. Well, naturally, people used to come out of the shop to see what had happened. An accident, eh? And there'd be my mate lying in the gutter.

'"Oh I'm not too bad," he used to say, "but I wouldn't half mind a drink." And then someone would go and get a bottle of something and he'd take a few mouthfuls and then further up the road he'd share what was left with the rest of us.

'And I remember, in the Dutch club championship, I was away with Wout Wagtmans. We were getting to the finish, just the two of us, when 500 metres before the line he saw this little children's bike in the crowd. So he jumped off, grabbed this children's bike, and finished the race on it.

'Laugh? I'd never seen anything so funny in my life.

. . . grabbed this children's bike, and finished the race . . .

'Unfortunately the judges didn't see it the same way and they disqualified the both of us, even though we were eight minutes clear.'

George Bernard Shaw was forever falling off his bike . . . or, more probably, off his trike.

'One afternoon in the middle of July,' he recorded once, 'I was riding in Pall Mall East when a Great Western Railway van, coming out of the Haymarket, turned up Pall Mall on its wrong side owing to the horse shying at something, and charged me point blank. It was a pretty piece of tournamenting. I went ahead gallantly, and hit the horse fair and square on the breastbone with my front tyre, fully believing that the most impetuous railway van must go down before the onslaught of Bernard Shaw. But it didn't.

'I hit the dust like the Templar before the lance of Ivanhoe; and though I managed to roll over and spring upright with an acrobatic bound just clear of the wheels, my bike came out a mangled, shrieking corpse. It was rather exciting for a sedentary literary man like myself.'

Such accidents weren't unusual. As the veteran peace campaigner, Bertrand Russell, recalled: 'Shaw and I were involved in a bicycle accident. . . . He was only just learning to ride a bicycle and he ran into my machine with such force that he was hurled through the air and landed on his back twenty feet from the place of collision.

'However, he got up completely unhurt and continued his ride; whereas my bicycle was smashed, and I had to return by train. It was a very slow train and at every station Shaw appeared on the platform, put his head into the carriage and jeered. I suspect he regarded the whole incident as proof of the virtues of vegetarianism.'

Johnny Hardcastle's mother viewed her son's occasional accidents with less literary merit.

'You are,' she'd scoff as Johnny staggered home, his knees shredded and his tracksuit black from its impact with the road, 'old enough to know better.'

Sadly, it was the cat that suffered. Sticking around out of sympathy for the blood-stained mess in front of it, it made an unmissable target for a rolled-up tub.

9.

How to be rather strange

Nobody could say why Amanda Lightbody was so different, so carefree, so . . . well, sexy, I suppose. What's more, it was very puzzling to see the way she gazed so fondly at Thighs as he shambled from one rather poor joke to the next during his club dinner speech. Frankly, as Johnny Hardcastle put it, her first three characteristics were all very welcome. But to see her with fluffed-up blond hair and a slinky, dark blue backless dress, making eyes at Thighs, was like watching pearls being cast before swine.

. . . his club dinner speech.

It was Back Wheel's theory that she'd discarded her anorak in the African bush, suffered from the sun, and had a wild romance with a pigmy. It had, he insisted, loosened her up and given her visions of Her True Self. Being half cut at the time, we discussed this theory at some length.

If it was true, Johnny Hardcastle said, we should avoid telling Mr Lightbody. Apparently there had been a downturn in the wet fish business and nobody had been round there for weeks in case it was true he was already having second thoughts about the amount of cod he could spare for the Golden Crispycod 10-mile Challenge. Sponsors like that weren't easy to find, he said, and the local paper hadn't been kind in helping with publicity: neglecting the company name but unfortunately referring to Mr Lightbody as 'a thrusting haddock tycoon'.

But the fact remained: where once it had been Thighs loping about after Mandy, his chin dropped and his brain struggling for a line of conversation, now it was Mandy wrapping her arms round his above the dinner table, and playing footsy beneath it. For a moment this caused a *frisson* of embarassment as Thighs, uncertain of where his legs would stray if they weren't strapped into his pedals, began footsying instead with Aubrey Fothergill, whose Freeman Hardy and Willis Everlasters stretched from the other side of the table.

The look in both their faces was worth seeing. Thighs looked puzzled, as anyone might on finding woolliness where he'd expected gossamer nylon. Aubrey, on the other hand, who's long since disproved that sex is hereditary (ie that if your parents didn't have it, then you won't either), adopted an air of elation and mystic satisfaction for the few moments he thought it was Mandy's rather than Sweeting's leg that was fondling his. The look of disappointment when he realised the truth was hard to describe.

In the weeks that followed, Thighs took Mandy to the Long Eaton Paragon freewheeling competition, a slide show of Corsica by ultra-keen tourists of the Burton-upon-Trent CTC, and once, by mistake (since they'd taken the wrong bus for the Nuneaton ring-road disco), to Lutterworth, where they ate Big Macs in the rain and gazed at each other soulfully. Not once did Mandy wear her anorak.

Sitting in the bus shelter at Lutterworth, Thighs kissed her properly for the first time and slid his hand inside her jacket and then inside the upper buttons of her dress. It took some doing, not because Mandy objected, but because Thighs wasn't very good at undoing buttons fastened the female way round. Only after several attempts, interrupted by buses delivering members of Lutterworth Granada Bingo Centre, did he hit target.

'Oh, Mandy,' he groaned.

'Yes?' Mandy whispered with tenderness.

'I . . . er . . . you . . . oh Mandy!'

He had discovered Mandy wasn't wearing a bra.

'You . . . I . . . er . . . gosh!'

This sudden but pleasant reacquaintance with school biology lessons left him too weak to attend the clubroom for several weeks. Next day he took Mandy more back-numbers of *Cycling* as a kind of thank you.

In doing so, he was following the kind of largesse to which successful racing cyclists are accustomed. It was a tradition for many years that the winner of the Tour de France gave all his prizes to his *domestiques,* the weary and occasionally brain-dead Big Legs who'd chased round France on his behalf. For Rik van Looy, this job entailed the frequent collection and delivery of bottles of beer (in the days when bar owners were seemingly delighted to have their fridges raided by cyclists of all nations). He could get through half a dozen on a long climb.

Among those required to do this kind of menial ferrying was a tall Cheshire man called Vin Denson. The foot or so difference in their height meant Denson could easily have stooped and crashed a waiter's tray on van Looy's bonce whenever he chose. But with van Looy, who had fingers in many pies, it was an idea best thought and not executed.

'Denson, I feel a bit sick. *Café snel!*' shouted van Looy in the Dauphiné Libéré. Denson groaned inwardly, detached himself from the bunch and stopped once again at a bar. As everyone else hurtled up the road, the unfortunate Denson rushed inside with his bottle and begged the café owner to fill it with coffee, as instructed. And there was the big mistake.

For mile after mile, the unwitting Denson chased back to the main field, worked his way up through a couple of hundred riders and, proud but exhausted, handed the coffee to van Looy. It was just what he'd want for his upset stomach, he thought.

The Great Man frowned as he took the plastic bottle. It was warm. Suspicious, he flipped open the plastic lid, sniffed the contents . . . and emptied them over the road.

'*Stommeling!*' he shouted. 'Idiot! I said café . . . bar . . . beer! I want beer, *jongen!*'

Suddenly Denson learned the hard way that *café* in Flemish – which he never learned – doesn't mean what it does in French. Dutifully and miserably, he stopped off again at the next bar. If the master wants beer . . .

While Denson was one of the largest riders in the game, Jean Robic was, at 5 ft 4 in, among the smallest. In 1947, he became the first rider to win the Tour de France on the last day, without having led it once. He was nearly three minutes behind the maillot jaune on the last stage, which everyone had expected to be a procession from Caen to Paris.

For some reason which nobody understands, least of all Brambilla, the leader, nobody chased. Robic finished the day 10:07 in front of him and won the Tour by seven minutes.

The point of telling this story is that since Robic didn't have the weight to take him down mountains fast, he arranged for a helper to wait at the top of climbs with a bottle of lead shot. This he'd fasten to his bike for the descent, keeping it low down to help his balance. Sadly, he died just a few years ago in a car crash.

The saddest story about drinking bottles, though, concerns another Frenchman, the world champion Antonin Magne, later a successful team leader. On one of the hottest days of the summer, Magne had been away for mile after mile, never quite catching a lorry which was throwing up clouds of dust. His throat was cracking from dryness.

Finally, suffering, but sure of victory, he saw a helper standing on a bridge, holding up a bottle. Gratefully he grasped for it. Sadly the helper let go too soon, the bottle dropped into his front wheel, and Magne was spreadeagled at not inconsiderable speed across the road.

Bottles passed up like this are not always innocent. Paul Duboc was a French carpenter who was doing the ride of his life during the Tour de France of 1909. He raced first into Perpignan, then first into

Luchon, and even dropped François Fabier, the big-hitter of the day. And then on the climb of the Aubisque, still going like a train, he suddenly went beserk, wobbled all over the road, shot down a goat track and ended up in a heap on the ground, spewing up his insides.

The astonishing thing about this story isn't just that Duboc had been given a dosed drink by a competitor called Lafourcade, who was disqualified for life as a result. It's that Duboc spent hours recovering in the goat track before finally getting back on his bike, crawling weakly to the stage finish and getting in four hours down. Despite all that, he still finished the Tour second on points.

Which is more than you can say of either Cyrille van Hauwaert or Abd el Kaader.

Van Hauwaert (who before he died at nearly ninety became one of Eddy Merckx's sponsors) once succeeded in winning Milan–San Remo after riding to the start (from Belgium, that is). Like van Looy, he also enjoyed a beer as he rode. In his first race in France he drank proffered wine in the same quantities, liked the taste, and, well . . .

'I finished completely drunk,' he said afterwards. 'I couldn't tell where I was going, in what direction, and of course I was far behind the others. I never touched wine again.'

Nor did Abd el Kaader. And yet the Tour legends tell that he was found drunk by the roadside and stinking of alcohol. This, of course, quite cheesed the old boy off because he was a Muslim and had dutifully followed Allah's guidance and never touched alcohol. The truth, from which legends are born, is that he'd collapsed with sunstroke and a passer-by had tried but failed to revive him by emptying a bottle of wine over his forehead.

If drink is a rider's undoing, coffee can be his salvation. It did, anyway, once come to Vin Denson's rescue. The longest road race of all is one of the oldest, from Bordeaux to Paris. It no longer has the romance and the importance that gave it the exaggerated epithet of Derby of the Road, but when Denson rode it was quite something.

Forgive me if you already know this, but Bordeaux–Paris starts in darkness down in the extreme south-west and for the first 150 miles or so the riders swish along the main road northwards, until dawn. Now, they don't hang about, but they do ride in tracksuits.

In 1965, there was the usual gentleman's agreement that the bunch would stay together until daybreak. At the agreed moment,

It's all right these days, when there are always team managers and hangers-on to hand up bottles of Coke and Perrier.
In the old days it wasn't so easy, and thirst could be a terrible problem on the dusty roads of the parched south.

Quite whether it was necessary to go to the lengths of
Marcel Kint is quite another matter, though. To get used to
the terrible pangs he'd feel later in the year, Kint – the world
champion in 1938 – left home for his training runs with a
shoulder bag of salted fish. Whenever he felt hungry, the
fish would sustain him and the salty thirst reminded him of
agonising days in the south of France.

the bunch pulled to a halt on wet roads and began pulling off its
rain-sodden clothing. At the back, though, the Frenchman Claude
Valdois had already done his changing as he rode, so that when the
others stopped, he attacked.

'He literally caught us with our pants down when he suddenly
jumped away,' says Denson, who was riding as *domestique* for
Jacques Anquetil. And this time the big chief was shouting not for
Denson to drop back but for Denson to get up the road after this
potential rival and get up there pretty damned quickly.

'I jumped after him with my shorts half on, fastening my braces,
and Stablinski, the other Ford man riding for Anquetil, followed with
one sock on and still trying to get his heels in his shoes.'

All this scrambling gave Denson two problems. First, the
chamois in his shorts had been greased and the rush meant gravel
from his shoes stuck to the cream as he pushed his shoes through
the legs. And second, of course, Denson hadn't had a pee since
Bordeaux, several hours back.

He caught Valdois just before Châtellerault, from where the last
200 miles are ridden behind little motorbikes. Taking a prize for
picking up his Derny motorcycle first, Denson and his pacemaker,
Pleasance, headed off towards Paris.

'I think he had rosy dreams of us winning the race,' says Denson.
In fact he couldn't, because he was there to defend Anquetil. And
for several more miles they spun along at 40 mph.

'We were five minutes up,' Denson told *Cycling,* 'when, in agony,
I could no longer ignore the insistence of nature and I called to
Pleasance to stop.

'"You can't stop in Bordeaux–Paris," he cried, to which I replied "Watch me!" and I lined up at a tree.'

Now, when Desgrange didn't want women on his Tour de France, it was problems just such as this that he envisaged. The French have an odd fascination (which after 1992 may become compulsory for all of us) in these *sujets biologiques* and as Denson unhitched his braces and pulled down the front of his shorts, he was immediately surrounded by journalists, television cameramen, race officials, his pacemaker Pleasance, his *soigneur* Bernard Stoops, and half a dozen passers-by delighted at a little commotion to break the early-morning tedium.

For five minutes he stood there, struck dry by nerves and hours in the saddle, the cameras whirring, the happy little crowd cheering and urging him on like a race horse. And all the time the lesser lights were droning past behind their little motorbikes, their fat old pacemakers looking ludicrous and sitting upright to shelter them.

Finally Anquetil swept into sight, already locked in his 200-mile battle with Tom Simpson, who was Denson's closest friend but also a dangerous rival because he rode for a competing team. With them was Stablinski. The last thing Anquetil had in mind when he signed Denson's pay cheques was that the Englishman would be stuck behind a tree, desperately trying to open the flood gates. Anquetil had only just finished the Dauphiné Libéré stage race and had started Bordeaux–Paris after only an hour's sleep. He needed Denson to nurse him, to cosset him, and sometimes even to push him.

Thirty miles later, Denson was forced to stop again. Happily, the cameramen rushed up again; Pleasance, Stoops, half a dozen reporters and a fresh set of passers-by all joined in, and again Denson strained against nature.

'This time I had an unrewarding three minutes,' Denson laughs, 'until the *soigneur* came up and did the trick with the aid of hot coffee on a sponge!'

Anyway, it was minnows like Denson who gained when their team leader won the Tour de France. Le Leader imperiously accepts the homage of his adoring public and then peels off the fivers in the changing rooms. The idea was that he'd collect so much in criterium contracts for the rest of the season that what he won in the Tour was as nothing. He could afford to be generous.

Frankly, I don't know whether the tradition continues as strongly

... the cameras whirring, the happy little crowd cheering ...

these days, because there is now a great deal more money in the
Tour for everybody (following a Communist newspaper's claims
years back that there were enough prizes to see that every sponsor
went home satisfied but half the riders stayed underpaid). Added to
that, there are fewer post-Tour criteriums than there were and a few
top riders, like Greg LeMond, don't bother to ride those that there
are.

Either way, I like to think that there's enough in it for the also-rans.
Among the traditions was that the last rider in the Tour de France
could be sure of as many criterium contracts as the winner,
although rather more poorly paid, of course.

The *lanterne rouge* is an unenviable character. The American
writer Jack Olsen said of him and his ilk in 1966 that he 'may have
lost his toenails from the constant forward pressure in his cycling
shoes, his backside may be pocked by suppurating ulcers and his

mind so addled by amphetamine that he is not sure of his name, but he is a hero, a major athletic figure, a finisher in the Tour de France, the most trying sports event in the world.'

Olsen was talking of what he called 'the touchy subject of goofballs'. And there's no doubt that 'goofballs' once did and perhaps still do play a big part in Continental cycling. It was no exaggeration to say you could pick out where a race had been in its last miles to the finish by the discarded pill wrappers and empty syringes. Riders died from it, and a few went mad enough to drive their cars at the race barriers afterwards, or drive round town shooting guns at lamp posts. It wasn't normal behaviour, even for drugged bike riders, but it's always the extremes that get remembered.

There was a time when the fame and fortune of winning just a stage of the Tour de France was enough to set yourself up in a small business, such as a garage or a bar. And that's all most riders aspired to. There isn't, after all, much satisfaction in running errands for the team leader except for the money that it brings.

As a result, many riders were prepared to dope themselves to the point of stupidity to achieve a success in their home region. People in the sport are still reluctant to talk about it but the truth, in those days before the dangers were realised, is that many riders spent their summers on dope and their winters on alpine holidays and carrot-juice diets to rid themselves of the dregs.

When Tom Simpson died in 1967, his death was induced by drugs. And yet Jacques Anquetil blamed his death not on dope but on dope controls. Tom hadn't used the right drug, Anquetil said, because he'd been afraid of being caught.

Of course, yet odder things happened afterwards. Riders became adept at dodging the early dope checks (euphemistically called 'medical controls'). One story going the rounds is that a Belgian rider who switched his wife's urine for his own was cleared of doping but pronounced pregnant. The fact that nobody can say who this rider was or precisely where it happened shouldn't be allowed to detract from the tale.

Fiddles like this certainly happened. The Belgian champion Michel Pollentier was caught at the top of the Alpe d'Huez with a rubber flask of urine under his armpit and a network of rubber tubing ending in the legs of his shorts. In that way he could pretend he was urinating when in fact he was defrauding the check. Pollentier was indeed drugged. That much was proved afterwards, of him and several other riders. But the most unbelievable part of the story is that Pollentier, probably the least gainly rider the sport has ever known, had just taken the race lead and was thus guaranteed a dope check.

It's something that Eric Caritoux must fear all the time, not because of pure stimulants but because the testing machines are now so sensitive that they pick up the slightest traces of offensive drugs in innocent medicines. And when it comes to medical troubles, our Eric holds something of a record.

He is, with a little exaggeration, allergic to almost everything. You wonder how he ever managed to become the French national champion in two years running – 1988 and 1989. He comes over all funny to dust, deodorant, red spiders, mites, olives and woollen mattresses. Quite a list. At home he lives with minimal furniture and all the windows permanently shut. He sleeps on a synthetic mattress. Not much of a life.

10.

How to be rich, famous and fabulously successful

There used to be people who asked you to send them £5 for a seat at the Cup Final. And then, just as you were setting out to buy your rattle and your Chelsea scarf (this was a long time ago, after all), what you got in return was a small folding chair. For the same reason, you should take no notice of books which have chapters offering to make you rich, famous and fabulously successful. And anyway, things like that don't always work out the way you'd want them.

Take Fausto Coppi, for example. Now, there was a chap of whom legends were made. He won two world pursuit championships, one world road title, five Tours of Italy, two Tours de France, four Italian championships, three Milan–San Remos and broke the world hour record. He also looked thin, unhealthy and emaciated and as if he'd just come out of prison camp – which, since we locked him up for being on the wrong side during the war, was actually the case.

I remember seeing a film of Coppi once. He was on a mountain climb, with a drop on one side and a rough rock wall on the other. There was the normal lock of oily hair over his forehead and he was riding ever upward with those familiar sunken cheeks, beaked nose and curved back. Behind him were a dozen or so riders strung out on his wheel, wishing he wasn't going quite so fast.

The point of the story is that Coppi has a bag over his shoulder from which he's transferring what look like prunes to his back jersey pockets. He has, therefore, only one hand on the handlebars and still he's got everyone lined out behind him. When the final prune has been safely ferried across, he throws away the bag, puts both hands on the handlebars and gets back to business. The other riders are promptly shot off the back.

Rides like that made him a legend, of course, and the Italians thought he was superb – which he was. Unfortunately, events took a curious twist and he left his wife and family and moved in with another woman. This would have been scandalous enough in those less permissive times, but the woman that Coppi chose was actually the one who lived next door.

Well, shock and horror. Coppi and the new mistress, quickly called the Woman in White for her curiously virginal choice of clothing, filled the papers of the day. Where once Coppi had been adulated, now he was cursed in the street and spat at.

In one tragi-comic episode, the Pope refused to bless the Tour of Italy while Coppi remained part of it. Coppi, I read once, was an atheist, so perhaps he wasn't too bothered.

In the end, I think they must have forgiven him. Not only is there a memorial to him on the Col de l'Izoard, but there's a much more spectacular one at the church at Castellania, a village about halfway between Genoa and Milan. It was there that Coppi was born, in a street now called Via Fausto Coppi. The house still stands.

Behind the church you'll find the marble tombs of Fausto and his brother Serse, who died in 1953 after his own career on the bike. Alongside are four 12-foot copper plaques listing Fausto's triumphs.

But more striking, perhaps, is the inside of the church. Because there, near the big wooden doors, hang world championship rainbow jerseys, trade team jerseys, national jerseys and Tour de France jerseys. They, along with simple club hats and photographs, have been left by unnoticed, unremarked ordinary visitors still anxious to keep the Coppi legend alive.

More than that, every year on the day before the Tour of Lombardy, it's a tradition to call at the chapel of the Madonna del Ghisallo, above the lake at Bellagio. Once upon a time, when the Tour of Lombardy was more of a race than it is now, the climb was a big feature. Before 1958, it was rough and unsurfaced and it played havoc with everybody. Coppi used it to split the field when he won four times on the run, from 1946 to 1949. It was forty miles, in those days, from the finish in Milan.

Whether the Vatican ever regretted it, I don't know, but in 1948 Pope Pius XII went along with Italian riders' suggestions and lit a candle in the chapel's choir stall. He made the Madonna the patron saint of racing cyclists and to this day you'll see hanging there the bike on which Coppi won the 1948 Tour de France.

This is in contrast to the bike on which Jan Janssen won the Tour in 1968. That, too, became famous because, until Greg LeMond's narrow win in 1989, it enjoyed the status of having won by the closest margin. (Janssen, who doesn't look a day older now than he did at the time, beat a doleful and hangdog Belgian called Herman van Springel in the closing time trial and the *maillot jaune* that he won was the only one he wore throughout the Tour.) Janssen's bike, far from being hung in some revered site, is carted around the countryside as a feature of trade exhibitions.

Even that was more glamorous than what happened to the machine on which Les West took one of his Milk Races. It was put on a stand at the Cycle Show in London and appropriately labelled. Within days, an anonymous caller had told the BCF that he was going 'to get West' and reported him for an alleged breach of the rules of amateurism.

West's Milk Races sound much more fun than they are now; either because there wasn't much money in the race wallet, or because the hotels hadn't got the hang of racing cyclists, and there was never enough to eat. Riders were given extra money to buy a further evening meal.

If you were in a town of no great distinction, this was fairly safe so far as the team managers were concerned. But unfortunately the Milk Race has always spent a lot of time trooping around seaside resorts, and team-loads of cyclists who'd been let loose at Blackpool, Brighton or Great Yarmouth ended up treating the place like medical students on rag days.

'We used to have Kenny Hill, Pete Matthews and Billy Perkins, three Scousers,' West told me once. 'And instead of being tucked up in bed, we were out on the town, in restaurants and having a laugh. We just used to be out on the town.

'And of course we were in the ruddy cafés and the restaurants at all hours. We used to go down in a taxi and then the buggers, they used to get out of the taxi and they used to all run off and say they weren't paying. And I'd have to pay the money.

'We went in Madame Tussaud's waxworks at Morecambe, in the

back entrance and got kicked out of there. And went in cafés and Pete Matthews never used to pay half the time. He used to sneak out, and the waitress used to say "If you can get out of here without paying, you're welcome to" and the bugger got out all the same.

'It was like a fortnight's holiday, really, except we had to work again next morning.'

The first time I met West was on the Isle of Man, when the cycling week there was really something. I was trying to persuade him to ride the Bessums 'Best for Radiators' End-of-Season Grand Prix. It was at one of those weeks that Johnny Hardcastle bought half a pint of lager for Rudi Altig, who was one of the international stars of the day. It was that same week when Johnny Hardcastle did two other memorable things.

The first was to climb off the ghost train at Onchan fun fair before the little railway car had re-emerged into daylight. This meant nothing to the ghost train operator, of course, who was much more concerned with getting people into the cars rather than out of them. To the friends of Johnny Hardcastle, on the other hand, it was very noticeable indeed, and before long we were all paying tenpence to take a ride through the tunnel to see what had become of him.

At first there was no sign. But on passing the tilted coffin which would normally have opened to reveal a skeleton, we were treated to Johnny Hardcastle sitting suddenly upright as the lid opened and screaming at the top of his voice.

This we all voted a tremendous hit. Johnny, of course, varied his routine by paying special attention to the girls. Accustomed as he was to the darkness, he could see them twisting their way towards him on the winding little railway. By the time they reached him, he was ready.

In the end, of course, he just went too far. My own feeling is that he showed considerable ingenuity, but the magistrates didn't agree. Instead of just sitting up and shouting 'boo', he made two girls cry by sitting up, shouting 'boo' and then hurling the plastic skeleton into their laps.

Most of the previous passengers had either enjoyed the joke or hadn't realised that Johnny Hardcastle wasn't just part of the show. Two trembling teenage girls getting back to the ticket office with one of the owner's plastic skeletons round their shoulders wasn't likely to go unnoticed, however.

Johnny was fined £10 at Douglas magistrates' court next

morning for causing a public nuisance. We all sat there in the public seats with our sandwiches and our damp capes, hoping it might be the birch (which in those days on the Isle of Man still flourished). But we were disappointed. Two weeks later the *Isle of Man Examiner* printed an editorial about Johnny Hardcastle being 'the kind of visitor the island could gladly do without'.

Johnny's only regret was that this unique stain on his record meant he had to miss the Castletown kermesse.

The kermesses, in an era when races on closed roads were a novelty, were the great success of Isle of Man week. The crème de la crème, though, were the tricycle races. The notion of tricycling is already sufficiently absurd, but a dozen or more of these uncontrollable creatures thundering like overgrown and unpredictable beetles through the narrow streets of Castletown and Ramsey was irresistible.

Nobody but the tricyclists cared who won, and nobody else ever knew, since all tricyclists have beards and wear caps and are therefore indistinguishable from each other. The only rider everybody knew was a chap with the words 'Dodgy Knees' painted prominently on his top tube.

Johnny was also one of several cyclists each night who realised, after rather too many drinks, that there was a picture booth on the main prom at Douglas. And outside those little booths, where you sit with the curtain drawn waiting for the flash, there are always strips of photographs of people who have been in earlier.

Johnny, alcoholically but logically concluded that it was somebody's job to go through all the negatives, therefore entered and took several pictures of his naked backside. This, he thought, was tremendously funny and certain never to have been done before. In fact, many years later I did meet just such an employee of the photo-booth company. He said the number of bare-backside pictures during cycling week was exceeded only by those he had to clear out during the previous fortnight's TT races.

Anyway, to get back to Les West for a moment, he had a certain talent for trouble. On one famous occasion, he turned up late at the start in Brighton and, as with anyone else turning up after the

. . . several pictures of his naked backside.

signing-on had finished, they told him he couldn't get a ride. Even today, he still feels offended by the absurdity of it all.

'I was working the day before,' he said. 'I mean, I was working [as a joiner] all the time. All the time as an amateur I used to have a full-time job and go training three times a week at night.

'We should have been there on the Friday and I didn't get picked up until Saturday dinner time. And of course we were a day late when we got to Brighton. We got lost going through London – me, Brian Rourke, Barry Lawton and the driver – so we just rolled up as innocent as anything and they said we couldn't ride.

'Well, that was the night before, so I don't know what all the fuss was about. We had a bit of an argument but the thing was you couldn't really argue too much. Bob Thom [the manager] told us to shut up and get out of the way, and they had a meeting.

'But they were going to say, right, half the team weren't going to ride. I mean, the Great Britain team were going to not ride. But I don't think they told the organisers that. That was going to be if the result had gone the other way.

'When I think about it, it's a bit stupid . . . all those daft things that went on.

'Can you imagine that on the Continent? I was one of the top riders in the race and they were going to stop me riding. I mean on the Continent they'd come and fetch me, wouldn't they? And when I got there they'd say "Well thank God you've turned up; you had us worried." But that's the difference. I laugh when I think about it now.'

But at least he finished. Which is quite in contrast to Percy Stallard. Percy – the man who single-handedly and almost inadvertently brought about the biggest row that cycling's ever known – didn't finish his first road race. That was in 1933.

The reason Stallard caused such a fuss is that, during the war, when the roads were empty because of petrol shortages, he held a road race from Llangollen to Wolverhampton. The cycling authorities were against it but Stallard thought that if he ran it, they'd see there were no problems. They might even feel grateful and see the light.

The race was a success, but they weren't grateful. In fact they banned Stallard for life and suspended everyone who'd taken part. Far from ending road racing, however, they'd blundered. Denied access to the NCU, Stallard and the rest had to form their own organisation – the British League of Racing Cyclists.

The battle between the NCU and the BLRC outlasted the war and ended, with road racing by then a fixture, with the amalgamation of the two into the British Cycling Federation.

Stallard, dismissing his status as the father of modern road racing, says that not only doesn't he rate what he did, but if he had his time all over, he'd never do it again.

'All you get,' he told me, 'is trouble from anarchists.'

In those days (pre-1933), you see, there hadn't been any road racing in Britain. There'd been a mix-up between a tricycle team time trial and a woman on a horse years before and the National Cyclists' Union had abandoned all racing on the road for fear that the police would ban cycling altogether.

As it happened, a group of rebels got together and formed what later became the RTTC. The notion that a body as august and traditional as the RTTC could ever have been run by a bunch of Che

Guevaras isn't easy to swallow in the 1990s, but that's the way it was. They got up before first light and ran individual races against the clock.

And that, with a little track racing, was the way it stayed in Britain until 1933 when the Charlotteville CC hit on the idea of running road races on the motor-racing circuit at Brooklands in Surrey. For the first time, a road race – this one – was going to be used to pick the team for the world road race championship. Until then, everyone had been chosen on his time-trialling ability, which was like choosing a chess champion on his skill at solving crosswords.

Stallard, a 24-year-old from Wolverhampton, entered. In 1933 no one had ridden a road race before and the whole sixty-three miles were like kick-and-rush football.

'You cannot teach time-trial Englishmen to change their tactics with a single race,' said *Cycling*, who put up a twenty-guinea trophy. 'Team co-operation was conspicuous by its absence.'

Ten thousand people stood in the rain to watch.

Part of the course was a hill used for testing the cars. It was one in four. And here the story takes on that pleasing note of absurdity which makes cycling such a cranky sport.

'On the first lap,' Stallard told me more than fifty years later, 'I pulled my foot out and I ran up. I was in the lead then and several other riders passed me. Well, I couldn't get back on my bike at that steep angle, so I ran past these other riders and won the prime at the top *running!*'

He quickly cottoned on that he could run up the hill faster than anyone else could ride, so for the next two laps he hopped off again, trotted up to the line, and collected the prime. In the end, a puncture put him out of the race, so it was his running ability, therefore, that got him a ride in the world championship.

'It's farcical, really. And another thing that happened . . . my tyre was going down. And I pumped it up – it wasn't flat – and got to the pits, and I'd just put a new front wheel in and the commissaire came racing up. "You can't do that, you can't do that; you've got to change the tyre."

'I had to take this wheel back out and put the tyre back on my own. That's how they did things in those days.'

In later races, riders had to change a tyre twice whether they'd punctured or not. It got so that Stallard could do it in a minute and ten seconds, including pumping by hand.

. . . won the prime at the top running!

Having won several primes, and since he seemed to know what
he was doing, Stallard was asked to ride for Britain in the next world
championship. It was only his second road race, and when he got
there he went training in khaki touring shorts and a brown shirt. The
foreign papers called him The Boy Scout. In fact the whole of the
national team was a bit of a hoot because they'd been sent into
battle with two-speed Sturmey-Archers, whereas everyone else had
derailleurs.

At Montlhéry, at the world championship, he finished eleventh,
despite crashing. It was the first road race he'd ever finished and
only the second that he'd started. Quite a man.

11.

How to survive life's little pinpricks

It was about eighteen months ago that Dutch Luuc came back for a second visit. The land of clogs and dikes had been kind to him and the matchstick legs had begun to flesh out a little. With the extra strength, he set about belittling Thighs Sweeting all over again in the Hemel Hempstead Hilly '25' and then carried on winning right up to and including the Bessums 'Best for Radiators' End-of-Season Grand Prix, in which he broke away right from the start with Thighs and then dropped him six miles later.

This, of course, didn't please Thighs at all, and it displeased Aubrey Fothergill even more. Aubrey was still smarting over the Race of Trooce incident, and halfway through the summer, when it was becoming plain which way the season was going, he tried to introduce a rule banning foreigners from the club championship. Even so, by September, he found himself handing over not only the Golden Crispycod Challenge Cup and the mandatory five packets of frozen fish, but also the Fothergill Trophy for best overall performance.

Never had a cup been more grudgingly parted with.

In the summer of 1989, Amanda Lightbody also started racing. She looked quite a picture, her long blond hair streaming and her miraculously slender legs turning with tempting prettiness. Never had so many hearts swooned from one end of the N7 course to the other. Hormones were hopping all the way from Duston to Little Brington and back. Like Eileen Sheridan, years previously, she had that ability to look composed even when she was knackered.

Unlike Johnny Hardcastle, who invariably looked knack-ered even when he was composed. His mother often remarked on this phenomenon and was told that, with prominent leg veins, scarred knees, and a funny sun-tan caused by long shorts and open-backed mitts, this look of being utterly drained is how a cyclist radiates good health.

If cyclists didn't have quite a different idea of normality from the rest of the population, they could never bring them-selves to walk round in track suits advertising other nations' haemorrhoid treatments. Those who fought a rear-guard action against absurd Continental trademarks gave up when an unkind manufacturer began selling rims label-led 'Durex'. From then on there was no point in further pro-test. When Back Wheel Ambrose bought a pair, he wasn't allowed to bring them into the house. Sylvie demanded he cover the offending word with tape.

In that way, Mandy was very much like another heart-breaker, the American girl Beth Heiden. In fact, Beth would probably object to being called a girl, but since she's little more than five feet tall and, at her peak, wore pigtails, I cannot think of a more descriptive word.

Anyway, Beth Heiden won the women's road race championship a few years ago on a bike about the size of a key ring. All over the world, cycling papers ran headlines about 'American Express', each one of them thinking it was the only one clever enough to have thought of it. Soon after winning, Beth got quite fed up with all the publicity and more than successfully hid away from everybody. Until she did, though, she broke the heart of all who gazed on her including, so it is said, the man who many years later became manager of the 7–Eleven professional team, Noël Dejonckheere.

Dejonckheere, equally baby-faced, won the world point championship in his youth, went to America on an invitation trip and liked it so much that he's been back and forth ever since. The 7-Eleven team, sponsored by a supermarket chain, was a mainly American team.

'Is it true you have a crush on Beth Heiden?' *Velo-news* asked him once.

Dejonckheere recognised the name but not the noun.

'What's a crush?' he asked.

Aubrey, as I remember, had expressed his disappointment that some unknown wag had scratched the silverware with a pin. The engraving now read rather wobblingly: 'The Aubrey Fothergill Memorial Trophy.' Aubrey, not only alive but hopping mad, wanted to resign on the spot. The only thing that stopped him was the hope that he'd be there next year to see Luuc lose and go home empty-handed. As it was, Johnny Hardcastle, on whom greatest suspicion inevitably fell, wisely found it best to avoid dark alleys for several weeks.

There was, in fact, an occasion on which one of cycling's most magnificent cups, the one for the BBAR winner, was discovered by a photographer from Cycling *being used by the recipient's children for making sand-pies.*

. . . for making sand-pies.

Beth's older brother was, at the time, one of those long-term students you only seem to get in the States. His name is Eric Heiden and at about the time Beth found the end of her rainbow, he was the greatest speed skater in decades. Geoffrey Nicholson, writing for *The Guardian,* said his not inconsiderable muscles made his skating skinsuit look like a sack stuffed with footballs.

In Czechoslovakia, waiting to interview Heiden myself, I found myself filling in time by re-translating him for the Czech press, to whom the fact that he was also a professional cyclist counted for nothing. A nation that didn't know Freddy Maertens wasn't going to show much interest in peccadilloes like Heiden spinning a few pedals for cash in his spare time.

'What do you do, Mr Heiden?' they asked.

'I'm going through class.'

'He's at college,' I said. 'He's a student.'

The Czechs, gathered in a cluster, wrote in co-ordinated bursts, the literary version of synchronised swimmers. It was impossible to tell if they were impressed or simply unmoved. There was a five-year quota for words and they were keeping their ends up.

'So what *did* you do?' a little bald man with glasses asked, switching tenses.

Eric looked as mystified as anyone in a nirvanic calm is ever likely to be.

'I've, er, always been a student.'

They wrote it down together: Always ... been ... a ... student. Full stop. And then they looked up like puppets pulled by a single hand.

'But you are a professional cyclist, no?'

They were genuinely puzzled.

'To get through college. And I wanna deal in real estate.'

I explained, because to Eric it seemed too obvious to be worth mentioning, that in America students paid to go through university. Not all schooling was free. That was a revelation and they wrote it down. And dealing in real estate meant buying, selling and making a profit out of land and people's houses. This was especially newsworthy, for they thanked me gravely again, looked at each other significantly, bowed their heads and wrote it down earnestly.

There was probably an editorial next morning on the iniquities of talented amateur sportsmen having to prostitute their talents and trade in the misery of the homeless, merely to secure an education. If there was, I don't know. And Eric, being such an easy-going guy, probably didn't care anyway. The last time I saw him was at Peterborough ice rink. He still looked as though he was made of footballs.

Anyway, the more Mandy Lightbody raced (that's what we were talking about several pages back, if you remember), the more Thighs trotted around lovestruck after her. Mandy was chipping whole minutes off her personal best times and her father, who'd been in Grimsby more than usual lately, would race across from the east coast in his Sierra with extra supplies of Golden Crispycod.

The poor chap was so tense after driving hard deals in the wet fish world that hours would pass before he'd stop talking to us like customers. He'd see Mandy's time, reduced by another big chunk, and start talking about percentages and discounts and on-going projected data extractions which would show how much better she'd be the following week. I think he liked this new world and especially this changed daughter. He was glad, I think, that she hadn't got the job on the *People's Friend,* and even – though perhaps he'd rather be spared the details – delighted that she'd been transformed by whatever happened in Africa.

He once even offered a whole case of frozen cod for a special women's championship, and Aubrey Fothergill had to point out tactfully that not only was Mandy the only woman in the race, but giving her packets of Golden Crispycod which probably already over-flowed the family refrigerator would be less than fully appreciated.

Unfortunately, the faster Mandy became, the more Thighs sacrificed his own career in her favour.

'Fast as you can, Mandy, that's all you've got to do', he'd grunt as knowledgeably and as tenderly as he could, still embarrassed to be seen in a girl's company. Or: 'It's a headwind going out, Mandy.' Or, standing by the roadside: 'Dig 'em in, Mandy'.

It wasn't advanced coaching, that's true, but little though Thighs realised, it no longer truly mattered. Love, they say, is both cruel and blind. The more time Thighs devoted to carrying her bags, posting her entries and waiting on the line with a warm drink, the slower his own times became. His eyes, his life, were just for Mandy, a sinuous, shapely, blonde and bra-less vision in a lime-green and pale blue skinsuit.

But women are cruel and fathomless creatures. And as Thighs became more and more devoted and so less and less speedy, so he became less attractive to her. And little by little it was clear that he had a rival.

For a while Mandy did her best to keep it from him. Like many riders blessed with the strength and sharp reactions necessary to be a sprinter, Thighs could show a temper. And sprinters crossed are best avoided. Reg Harris, the best sprinter we ever had, once entertained all who watched by emptying a cup of tea over the suit of a reporter from the Press Association. The poor chap had somehow displeased Harris with his scrivenership.

And hot drinks, curiously enough, were at the root of an even greater burst of temper concerning a 27-year-old chap called David Lantenberg. Lantenberg was the man who sold drinks at the track in Newark, New Jersey, while overseas the rest of the world was engaged in the First World War. This was nothing to be sneezed at, for American tracks in those days were so packed that if you dropped a penny from the sky, it wouldn't hit the ground. There was a lot of money to be made and it was well worth Lantenberg's while coming across from Brooklyn.

> *Henri Viaene, the hot-dog king of Belgium, made a mint from the catering at six-day races and football matches. He piled up so much in the way of profits that he was able to buy his own six-day track at Charleroi.*

In the afternoon, the track wasn't so crowded because the races were later that day and only a few hundred people had shown up to watch the riders train. With few people feeling thirsty, Lantenberg busied himself screwing up posters for those who'd follow that evening. Unfortunately, the screws kept popping out and rolling on to the track, where they began puncturing the riders' tyres. This alerted first the advertising manager and then the boss himself, Floyd MacFarland, who as well as running the track was also a riders' manager. MacFarland had a vile temper and set about inflicting it on the tea-and-bun man.

'Get the hell outta here,' he bellowed.

It wasn't an even match. Lantenberg had difficulty seeing over his tea counter at the best of times, and MacFarland was a giant.

'Nail any more of those up and I'll throw you out the track personally,' MacFarland raged, his habitual bowler hat shaking with anger.

'Push off,' Lantenberg yelled back, roughly level with the fob-watch in the manager's waistcoat. 'I gotta right.'

'The hell you have,' MacFarland hollered back, and a shoving match started.

Now, at this point, those looking on would have found difficulty getting bets against MacFarland winning. But the manager had made one vital miscalculation. Lantenberg, after all, had been screwing up posters. His hand still held the screwdriver, and within moments the be-suited MacFarland was staggering back like an elegant unicorn, the blade five inches into his head. He died that night in Newark city hospital.

If it's any consolation, Lantenberg was as desolate as anybody. The police charged him with assault, then murder and finally manslaughter. I wish I could tell you why, but I can't; all I can tell you is that he got off.

Those old track races were often the biggest gatherings in town. Nowadays, of course, the men in sharp suits head for the Wonderful Sound of Radio One. But in those days when they wanted to plug a song, they employed singers to go and warble at people queueing up peacefully to get into bike races. As you stood there, people dressed in bizarre outfits came and sang songs at you. They then gave you a slip of paper with the song's name on it and hoped you'd go off and buy the sheet music.

At the biggest meetings, you could be regaled every hundred yards by troupers determined to out-sing, out-dress or simply out-volume their neighbours. The biggest attraction of the lot, for the song-pluggers, was Madison Square Garden in New York, and on August 1, 1920, with the World War over, a group of entrepreneurs signed a deal to hold six-day races there.

See a six-day now and all you get is amplified pop music (except at Rotterdam, where you get pop competing with odd ethnic bands of Dutch traditionalists, who wander through the seats and knock your Coke over as they play discordant oompah music. The Dutch call it atmosphere and sit there smiling nervously, worrying it might mean they'll be charged extra).

At Madison Square Garden, though, the crowds were so vast that there were four full-sized bands all playing different tunes, one at each end of the back straight, one at each end of the finishing straight. People like Bing Crosby, who could never get rid of song-pluggers, turned up to watch. Word had it that he used to wait for a really good pile-up and then paid for the first aid. He was rarely disappointed.

A rider called Dan Pischione died when a track splinter stabbed him in the stomach; a whacky Australian called Reggie MacNamara once left a tooth embedded in the track after being fetched off.

Many of his troubles MacNamara brought on himself. His star act was to turn straight down the 45-degree banking and ride head-first into his cabin. It was only made of wood and of course it splintered. Sometimes MacNamara did as well, and he'd end up in hospital. When he did, he had one stock retort for reporters: 'Bloody silly sport, anyway, isn't it?'

MacNamara made his money mainly in America, but the Europeans taunted him that the American 'sixes' were soft. MacNamara often finished them not on the track but in a hospital bed, but all the same he was still a pretty good rider. When he took one European contract, it was to answer the jibes.

Charlie Ruys, who revived the London six-day, wrote of him: 'So over he came, to Berlin of all places. There the six was a very important one in those years. The crowd was very partisan, the field was the best one could find in 1926.

'Reggie arrived with his mate Harold Horan, rubbed it into all his opponents that they were wise to accept that the best team was now over from the States, that he would save them a little, that he would not ride them all into the ground, that he would even allow them to finish in the same lap, so long as nobody ever tried to double-cross him.

'They found out after a few days that the Iron Man meant business and so they accepted the visitors' victory, Mac and Horan winning on points from Rieger–Giorghetti, Hahn–Tietz, Sawall–Tonani and De Wolf–Stockeleyns. The rest were all well down.'

When Ruys re-started the London six-day at Earls Court during the sixties, I went every day and lived on hot dogs for a week. Henri Viaene would have been proud of me.

We, of course, had never ridden even a half-hour madison. Back Wheel had once fallen off in a handicap at Coventry and had never gone back again, and Johnny Hardcastle used to carry Thighs' wheels about in the track centre at Leicester (where he swore he was the only person not wearing a blazer). But that was about it.

Dutch Luuc, naturally enough, was different. In fact, by now it wasn't only Aubrey Fothergill who was getting rather sick of him. It was all very well making a monkey of us in everything we rode, but Dutch Luuc, it transpired, had even been offered a ride in the amateur six-day at Ghent.

It happened because of a week's trip he'd organised for us all to Rotterdam. And there, at a track puzzlingly called Ahoy, he'd done rather well one Sunday morning and caught a few eyes. Not least among these, we noticed, were Amanda's. Thighs couldn't get time off work and Mandy, who was still being kept quite well by the profits of the wet fish trade, had been suspiciously happy to go without him.

At any convenient moment, the two of them sloped off together. Even when we were together, they were inseparable. Whether Thighs had pictures of Mandy topless at Skegness we never found out, but he certainly had one of her topless at Zandvoort because Johnny Hardcastle, thoughtful to the end, took one of her and passed it on to him. She looked wonderful. And draped across her shoulder was a spindly arm attached at the other end to Dutch Luuc.

Later that year they went together to Ghent, and Dutch Luuc came much further down the results than he'd hoped. With persistent tact, Johnny Hardcastle sympathised pointedly and inquired why. Mandy blushed a lot and Luuc was overcome with unaccustomed language difficulties and claimed he couldn't explain properly in English.

Johnny himself, of course, had never travelled far in love. He is wise, for women are things of dark temperament.

A stage race in the north of England many years ago was livened up no end by the rumour that one of the best rider's wives had threatened to leave him if he rode. I forget the details, but the essence was that it was a bank holiday and that disappearing to do battle on a bicycle was the last of presumably many straws. Things like this are enormous fun to everyone who's not personally involved. Most bike riders, being rather heartless types from years of riding into headwinds, have long enjoyed the misery of others. Mending a puncture by the roadside, for example, takes longer in direct proportion to the number of people looking on, giving useless advice and making barbed comments of considerable severity.

But it's not quite as funny when it suddenly dawns on you that the man who's home could soon appear as an echoing cavern is the very bloke who's giving you a lift back home. And, since we had all met at his house and left our cars there, there was no escape.

For mile after mile through the darkness, our man sat behind the wheel silently, his long and laconic features made even more glum by the eery green light of the dashboard and the oncoming headlights. In these circumstances, it is very difficult to strike up a lasting conversation.

When the time came to draw up to his house, the place was dark and quiet. So was our driver. Like mourners at the deceased's front door, we trooped in silently behind him, our heads bowed. When we found the main power switch, for the electricity had been turned off, the house had been stripped. There were no curtains, no carpets, no lampshades. Instead, piled in the kitchen, were just two of everything: two knives, two forks, two plates, two cups, two saucers and two pans. She'd stuck to her word.

I told this story some time later to Back Wheel Ambrose. He just shrugged and looked even more slump-shouldered.

'No chance of that happening to me, I suppose?' he grumbled, with just a flicker of hope. Married to Sylvie, I think I might have felt the same.

The inevitable happened eventually, of course. On a damp day in August 1989, there was another wedding. Johnny Hardcastle was the best man, having ridden a '25' that morning and gone straight to the church, again puzzling the cat.

. . . no curtains, no carpets . . .

Mandy looked gorgeous and Dutch Luuc in a dark suit
resembled nothing more than a rolled-up umbrella. You can see the
photographs of them all even now, the photographer's flash glaring
off Sylvie's glasses as she stands behind Mandy, trying to be
mistaken for a bridesmaid. Next to her are several weather-beaten
men with ruddy, sea-stained faces, standing slightly clumsily in ill-
fitting brown suits, their caps screwed up in nervous hands. Out of
focus in the background, you can just make out the words 'Golden
Crispycod – As Fresh as the North Sea'.

Three clubmates (the fourth not having shown up, but later
sending his apologies) are standing awkwardly in the church
doorway, trying to hold an arch of wheels. Unfortunately, one of
them is the schoolboy champion, who later sees his wheel banging
along the road with other items tied to the bumper of the happy
couple's car.

Having ridden to the church, he has to padlock the rest of his
bike to the church railings and walk three miles home in the rain.

Of Thighs Sweeting, there was no sign. The last we heard, he'd
become a member of the Fenland Clarion.